Sacred SUFFERING

The Face of Ruthless Persecusion in Eritrea

100% of the proceeds from the sale of the book will go to help the persecuted church in Eritrea.

Sacred Suffering

The Face of Ruthless Persecusion in Eritrea

Hanibal Daniel

Translation by Yisacor

Sacred Suffering

Published by: Nehemiah International Ministry

Printed in Unites Stated of America

ISBN: 978-0-578-43922-8

Cover Photo: Esayas Zerazion

Cover and interior design: beteZION
info@betezion.com
www.betezion.com

Many of the people in the story are still alive. Some of the officers mentioned who were in Sawa, Wia, and Meitir are still in the army, possibly in the same positions they held during the time of the story. To ensure the safety of people in the story, names of major participants have been changed.

Thanks to

- my wife Senait Semereab who was the impetus to writing the book,
- the reviewers, who spent countless hours providing valuable editorial input, especially to Galen and Kristen Burleigh, Sara Bioleti, Berhane Meskel, Futsum Libanos and Dr. Nahor Haddish,
- the wonderful graphics and arts support in providing the cover design, especially to Ermias Zerazion,
- to all the interviewee's who shared their stories of suffering and persecution.

Contents

Dedication

To the martyrs and those who are in prison for HIS sake.

Remember those who are in prison as if you were their fellow prisoner, and those who are ill-treated, since you also are liable to bodily sufferings.

Hebrew 13:3 AMP

Foreword

The true story documented within the pages of this book highlights the amazing perseverance of a beautiful young woman. She willingly suffered ongoing persecution even though it cost her so much: her youth, health, higher educational opportunities, and a chance of family and a successful career. The account of her struggle is so compelling that readers will find it hard to stop reading until the very end. Ultimately, the fact that the story of this young woman, Aster, is not yet resolved will capture the reader's attention and at the same time will cause persistent curiosity of what comes next.

The degree and intensity of her ongoing persecution is hard to comprehend, especially when put in the context of Western life and its relative ease and comfort. The amazing reality is that relief for Aster was as close and available to her as signing a single piece of paper. But the act of signing that paper carried the weight of her eternal destiny as it would deny the reality of what her Redeemer did to secure her salvation. That reality was more compelling to her than the ease and relief that would come with her signature.

Aster's intellectual and academic capabilities were substantial as evidenced by her perfect score on the Eritrean High School Leaving Examination. It stands to reason that her signing of the faith-denial consent would have allowed her to pursue a successful career. This success would have given her a happy and comfortable life and attained for her a high level of respect and admiration in society. However, Aster fully realized and embraced that signing that paper would have led to misery and risked her eternal salvation. The reader will be drawn in to see whether this young woman reached a breaking point and denied her faith to secure her temporal relief and freedom from prison.

Unequivocally, she chose to be mistreated along with her Christian brothers and sisters rather than to enjoy the fleeting pleasures of a fallen world. She regarded her own shaming for the sake of Christ as greater value than the treasures of Eritrea because she fixed her eyes on her eternal reward.

Her bold personal testimony was further enhanced by her commitment to living a pure life. Her physical beauty caused her to be the target of her captors who tried to take advantage of her numerous times. She resisted with courage and suffered the painful consequences of that resistance.

While she suffered in being detained, she also had to deal with the loss of her beloved father. Through her grief, she held steadfastly to her faith even though her persecution persisted. The reader will be astounded at how the immense grace of God kept the soundness of her mind absolutely intact.

It is important to remember that this heartbreaking but

uplifting story is not only about Aster. It also serves as a reminder of the faith of so many others in Eritrea whose names are eternally and majestically engraved on the indestructible tablet of the "Hall of Fame of the Ancient Ancestral Faith." This special group includes Freweyni, a nurse whose audacity in the face of danger should be lauded to the utmost degree. Sister Freweyni took her life into her own hands and risked it by leaving her own young child behind to enable Aster to visit her grieving mother and sister. This happened during one of Aster's hospital transfers when she was suffering from the harsh treatment she received at Wae, a gruesome place known for its unrelenting and torturous temperatures.

This book is a must read for every Bible believing Eritrean and Christians everywhere for the following reasons:

1. The content of this book is a timely message and wake up call for believers around the world who are more caught up in the affairs of this world than in interceding in prayer on behalf of Christian brothers and sisters who are truly suffering under persecution.
2. The resilience and perseverance of these persecuted believers and martyrs in Eritrea should serve as a tremendous source of encouragement. This should motivate prayer warriors to continue to steadfastly stand in the gap for their fellow believers who are excruciatingly suffering for their faith. It should also cause great rejoicing and thanksgiving when they consider their commitment to prayer in previous hours of desperation and God's unfailing faithfulness.
3. The suffering described in this book should be seen as part of God's redemptive plan and serve as a challenge for believers to contemplate where they stand in their allegiance to Christ. This account should prompt the

crucial question for each of us: if Aster and her fellow suffering brothers and sisters were willing to risk it all for the sake of the cross of Christ, what about believers everywhere in the twenty first century? What are we willing to sacrifice when trials and adversity arrive at the doors of our preoccupied lives? May our Heavenly Father find us faithful!

To God, who is not willing to share His glory with anyone, be incomparable majesty and glory forever for the sustaining of His grace that was demonstrated in the courageous lives of Aster and her companions whose names are held in high honor in the celestial City, the New Jerusalem. Amen!

Futsum Libanos
Nehemiah International Ministry
Board Member

1

My Trip to *Sawa*[1]

Dear and beloved sisters and brothers,

May Grace and Peace from God the Father and Our Savior Jesus Christ be with you. I extend my greetings from this place of my imprisonment. Thanks to your continued support through prayer, my brothers and I still enjoy the grace of God, rejoice in hope, are patient in affliction, and still hope in the Saviour's goodness.

From the perspective of reason, our situation is most difficult, and since you are acquainted with it, it is not necessary for us to go into details. However, as the Apostle Paul says, "I am able to do all things through Him who gives me power."

My brothers and I, due to God's presence and power, have conquered our sufferings and distress. We wish nobody to

1 Sawa is a military training camp in Western Eritrea established in 1994. Since then, Sawa has received 30 intake of trainees through to 2017.

come here to the place of our imprisonment, not even our enemies, or even wild beasts, let alone our friends. However, like the Apostle Paul as he was led to his death, we "rejoice in the Lord." Likewise, putting our eyes on the joy ahead of us and watching the author and the perfecter of our faith, we rejoice in Him, and in endurance we bear our sufferings and troubles.

I started following the Saviour when I was still young. I loved Him from the outset. It is for this reason that I say I have followed Him for all my youth. I can't forget the things I learned at Sunday school. I believe the foundations of my faith were laid at that time. I especially remember a hymn we sang at Sunday school. It goes like this: "No persecution, death, trouble or suffering will separate me from the love of my Saviour, the Lord Jesus." Yes, even if the place of our incarceration is dark and difficult to live in, it can't take me away from the Saviour who loves me.

From a young age, I had a strong desire, ambition, and dream to become a highly trained pediatrician. The grace of God supported me, and I worked very hard to realize my dream. I completed my high school and finished at the top of my class almost every year. It was inevitable that I should go to Sawa after I completed Grade 11. For high school students after completing grade 11, their last year of high school is completed in Sawa, the military camp, where they do military as well as academic training.

As I prepared to go to Sawa, my Christian friends and I continuously prayed for God to shower His grace on us, that He might give us His Spirit abundantly to be faithful to Him in all circumstances. We knew that many Christians in Sawa had borne a lot of sufferings. As a result, we encouraged one another so difficulties would not dishearten us. We reminded one another to believe in God and supported one another.

Near the time of our departure, a get-together party was organised for my class to see us off. I attended the event with my classmates in the same hall. It was a wonderful time.

At the time, a funny classmate called me by name and jokingly gave me some advice. "Aster, keep your Christianity to yourself. Especially, remember not to carry the Bible with you to Sawa. My brother, like you, is a *pente*[2] (a derogatory name for Christians in Eritrea; it is short for Pentecostal). Mother very clearly warned him, 'Listen, child. Your Bible will leave you at the mercy of these monsters. Leave your Bible behind.' He didn't listen to her. Now, he is still languishing in prison. Listen, these people are cruel and do not have the fear of God. You better keep your faith to yourself." He spoke out of concern for my well-being.

My mother and my sister prepared things for me. I saw my eldest sister, Yerusalem, remove the Bible from my luggage. I angrily asked her why she removed my Bible and told her to replace it immediately.

Yerusalem had borne a lot of suffering for the sake of the Lord. She understood why I was angry and calmly said, "Please, be calm, and don't be angry. Don't you see we should be 'as shrewd as the snake and as innocent as the dove', as the Lord said?"

She then told me how she used to read the Bible in places where she could not do so legally. My sister and I started to rip the Bible out of its cover the whole night. Dawn arrived before we had proper sleep. My friends and I departed for Sawa in the morning, as it happened previously with the other rounds of

2 Short for *pente*costal, the government and its adherents use the term to refer to protestant Christians. In their use, the term takes the meaning of 'foreigner' and 'new comer,' and therefore one that doesn't belong to the old Christian tradition in the country.

students.

I said goodbye to my family and friends, and I boarded the bus. I was weeping profusely. My heart was filled with affection for my family, and I began sobbing. A young lady who sat beside me did the same. She comforted me, "Please, don't cry. We will be there just for a short time."

The bus started and, for a short distance, silence reigned in the bus. The young woman who sat beside me bowed her head and began to sob loudly. In turn, I began to comfort her, "Please don't cry." However, she would not be comforted, and I began to pray for her that God would give her strength and His peace.

"Sister, what is your name?" I asked her to get acquainted with her. She quietly told me her name. Trying to distract her from her tears, I began to tell her of my school life and the life I led in my neighbourhood.

In turn, she told me about herself. In the middle of her story, tears began rolling down her face. I thought she had some problem that troubled her.

"Look," she said, "I was born in *the-field*[3], in *Sahel*[4]. Eritrea was liberated when I was only 5 months old in 1991. My three brothers and I came to live here in Asmara. However, we lived a life quite different from our expectations. My father had wounds and was disabled during *the armed struggle*[5] years.

---

3 The Eritrean armed struggle against Ethiopia started in 1961. Since then, Eritreans have referred to the struggle or the battlefield as 'the-field.' 'People were born in the-field' (meaning in a place under the control of the Eritrean fronts) or 'Young people went to the-field' (which meant that they joined the struggle against Ethiopian occupation).

4 Sahle (a mountainous part of the country) was one of the nine districts in Eritrea and a stronghold of the Eritrean People's Liberation Front, which formed the government after the liberation of the country in 1991.

5 Ethiopia annexed Eritrea after the latter abolished the Federation (in 1950) imposed by the UN on the Eritrean people in 1962. The Eritreans started an armed struggle to gain their independence from Ethiopia in 1961, which they were unable to secure peacefully.

Therefore, he was demobilized shortly after independence. Everyone in the family started contributing to our income so that the family could lead a decent life. Despite his disabilities, my father and my brother, who was a *national service*[6] man, went to the frontline when war broke out again between Eritrea and Ethiopia in 1998."

She started sobbing again. She didn't finish her story. Students who sat near us began to speak to her, comforting her. I hugged her and joined her in her sobs and weeping.

"My father and brother were killed in the Third Offensive [i.e. 2000], and grief filled our home," she said, and she continued sobbing. That was not all. When life became tough, my other brother dropped out of school and found work. His effort really helped. However, because he had not gone to Sawa and hadn't received military training, he worked secretly and made sure that the military police didn't arrest him."

"One day, there was an intense round-up. My brother thought all was well and started home late at night. On his way, some soldiers stopped him and asked him for a pass [a piece of official paper that showed he was in the National Service]. He told them he had forgotten it at home and tried to convince them to let him go. However, they were not willing to listen to him and took him with them. Our home, which had started to recover [from economic hardship], was plunged into darkness again. My mother was at the end of her wits. She went and informed the administrator of our area of her problems. But he could not help her in any way."

"Mother developed diabetes and high blood pressure as a result

---

6 In 1994, the Government of Eritrea issued National Service, a decree that required 6 months of military training and 12 months of development related service of every Eritrean aged 18 and above. Any one who is in the National Service is called national service man/woman.

of the stress at home. My brother returned home a year and eight months later without the permission of his commanders on his way to his new duty station. The situation at home compelled him to remain in Asmara. As a result, he did not return to duty. Then, he started working secretly. However, three months later, his commanders sent some soldiers to our home and took him away. After sometime had passed, he attempted a cross-border emigration in vain. Now, he is still in Wia."

As she told me her story, I prayed: "O God, when will you bring our shame to an end?"

"My other brother" she continued, "had a belief that nothing good could come out of his life as long as he stayed in Eritrea. If anything good was to come out of his life, he believed he had to leave the country. Therefore, he gave Mother no rest until she paid for his immigration, borrowing money from relatives. He and my cousin together went to the Sudan."

"In the Sudan, once again, he asked for more money and pestered Mother, for he and my cousin had decided to go to Libya and on to Italy. Another cousin paid for their trip, and they safely arrived in Libya. As they tried to cross to Italy in one of the perilous boat crossings, unfortunately, my cousin, the only son to his mother, was tragically drowned. My brother made it to the shores of Italy."

I was heart-broken by the story, and my spirit was inconsolable.

Suddenly, the driver announced a stop and told us if we so wished, we could leave the bus and get fresh air for ten minutes.

2

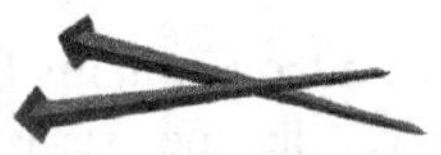

The Beginning of Temptation

We arrived at Sawa after dark. I didn't realize how quickly dawn arrived since I was very exhausted and slept like a log. As whistles began to be blown from every direction, we woke up, terrified. We arrived at the assigned meeting place since we had to obey the command of the military instruction. The commander took the stage, and everyone became quiet.

"As of today," the commander addressed us, "you are not only students but also soldiers. Therefore, you must show responsibility and accomplish the requirements of each duty very seriously. Everyone is expected to live here with due obedience. There is one more thing I want to stress strongly. This is a camp, not a church or a mosque. We know many of you come here carrying a Bible. Therefore, we want everyone who has a Bible to hand it over to the person assigned over you. However, if someone decides, 'I will hide my Bible and read it or preach secretly', let him or her be informed that we take this offence seriously and will enforce serious consequences."

He spoke in an angry tone and in a terrifying manner. I felt fear gripping my heart. However, a voice in my heart responded, "My heart, be not terrified. Girdle yourself with boldness." The voice I heard in my heart was stronger than the voice of the commander and overwhelmed it and made me forget his anger and boasts.

About a week after we came to Sawa, my friend, Rahwa, came running. Rahwa, a believer like me, was one of my closest friends. Both of us came from Asmara and shared our faith. As close friends, Rahwa and I shared our secrets and are like sisters.

"Have you heard? Have you heard?" she asked panting.

"What is it? Tell me!" I asked her, compelling her to tell me the news quickly.

"They have searched the males' living quarters" she told me.

"What are they looking for?" I asked.

"The Bible."

"And so what happened?"

"They collected some Bibles, and some submitted their Bibles voluntarily."

To encourage her I said, "The word of Christ is in our heart. Who can take it from us?"

She answered me, crying, "Can you believe it? It would have been good if they had put the Bibles in some place. They have put the Bibles in sacks so that they may burn them. Who, in their right mind, would burn Bibles?"

She was very angry and enraged.

Though I felt terrible, I told my friend, "Don't be discouraged! They cannot search, find and burn the Christ in our heart."

I tried to comfort her according to the grace God gave me.

"You know what? I have also heard they will search the female trainees' quarters. I think we should hide our Bibles in some secure place," my friend suggested.

I told my friend the experience of my elder sister. I told her that she tore out pages of the Bible and used them wisely when she was not allowed to read it legally. We agreed to do so. After one month, they burned all the Bibles they had confiscated from students. As for me and my friends, we continued reading my Bible by passing chapters from one person to the other, according to the wisdom God gave us.

One day, Rahwa came, her eyes puffed up and red with tears.

"Rahwa, are you alright?" I asked her. She didn't answer me because she was weeping. I gave her water to wash her face. Having just prepared it, I also gave her *tihni*[7]. After she had drunk the *tihni* and had calmed a bit, she told me that a fellow student had died in the camp.

I screamed so loudly that it looked as if the roof would fall on us. She came and shut my mouth with her two hands. In the middle of my tears, I asked her what caused our fellow student's death.

She told me, "He came late to the line. The man in charge ordered that he be punished in the scorching sun. He lost

---

7 In Eritrea, when National Service trainees leave for Sawa, their military training camp in western Eritrea, they take *tihni*, a kind of food which is consumed after it has been mixed with sugar in a semi-liquid form. *Tihni* is prepared by roasting barley and having it ground into a flour, removing the chaff with a sieve. It is a fast food which trainees can prepare in a short time as they leave for training early in the morning.

consciousness, and his heart could not function due to the excessive heat. Though they rushed him to the hospital, he was already dead when he arrived there."

My heart was filled with sadness, and my spirit was inconsolable. I knew the dead boy well as we lived in the same neighbourhood. He was the only child to his mother. His father had died while he was only a young child.

His mother was a hairdresser, and she brought him up while struggling to make ends meet. If she heard about his death, she would surely lose her mind. Thinking about the impact this would have on his mother, I found his death hard to bear. I vented my complaint, "Oh, God, a child is supposed to study at home, living among his family. Why do the Eritrean students, like soldiers, have to live in the forest and be treated cruelly?"

This was not the first time an incident like this happened. About a month before, another student had died among a line of students. For a moment, I thought about my fate.

We completed our first semester. I, with God's grace, scored above 95% in all the subjects that I studied. One day, while I was in the middle of a chat with my friends, I heard my name called loudly. It was the man in charge of the female trainees. He insructed that I should come to his office at 1 pm the next day. [In Sawa, the commanders used the same quarters as their home and offices. Commanders had no separate places for offices and living quarters. Therefore, this was his home and at the same time his office.] The manner in which the instruction was given shocked me and my friends. The sun is brutally hot at 1 PM in Sawa. It is hard to imagine unless experienced personally.

I could not ask such innocent questions as, "Why am I wanted? Is there something wrong?" Terrified, I agreed with a nod.

Then, I left my friends to go to review my notes. I could not do that either.

My mind was tense with perplexing questions. "Why does he want me in his office?" "Is it because of my Christian faith?" "What does he want from me?"

The next day one o'clock came, and I went to his office according to the appointment given me. I was trembling from fear.

3

An Appointment with the Colonel

As I came to the door, I heard a rough voice: "Hey cutie, may I help you?"

I answered, "Colonel Tecle asked me to come to his office."

The young man said, "Is that so? Oh yes, I remember, yes, yes. Follow me." He led me to Colonel Tecle's place which rather looked like a house. I said to myself, "This place doesn't look like an office. It looks like a residence."

I entered the house and stood in the middle of the living room. No one was there and suddenly I heard, "Asmarino[8], why are you standing? Have a seat." It was Colonel Tecle, and that brought me out of my daydream.

So I sat on what looked like a sofa.

---

8 Asmarino: colloquial for a city person, originated from Asmara - the capital city of Eritrea.

"What would you like to have? We have everything here!" he asked me, boasting. I shook my head and said, "I am full. I have already eaten my lunch."

He said, "No, I won't accept 'No' for an answer. You must eat something." Then, he shouted a name loudly. And a young lady came from another room quickly, "Yes, Colonel? What can I do for you?" she asked politely.

When I saw the young lady, my heart nearly jumped out of my chest. I felt very dizzy. I felt fear grip my heart.

Sometime ago, I was introduced to her. Though we were not classmates, I often saw her at school. She was a relative of my friend. My friend told me a number of stories about what happened to her here at the camp, which I had found hard to believe. But, now I knew and began to understand.

This beautiful young woman, whom Colonel Tecle asked to wait on me, was the center of attention at school in Asmara. Almost every male student wanted her for his girlfriend. At the camp [Sawa], the camp commanders and some students bothered her a lot. She was hunted like a bird. She had a great deal of interest in her education. Her parents were well to do, and she had easy access to any material she needed for her schooling.

And now, I saw her waiting on guests in the house to which I was invited. I prayed silently so that I would not have the same fate. The colonel was surprised when he saw us greeting each other.

"Did you know each other before? That is good," he remarked. He then quickly went on to ask me, "How is school?"

I answered him in a low voice, "It is fine."

The colonel then asked me, "Do you drink coffee?"

I answered. "No, I don't."

"You don't make coffee for your mother?" he said.

"Yes, I do."

"So, it means that you will make me a special coffee?"

He laughed aloud.

"O God, please don't deliver me into the hands of these cruel people!" I prayed.

"Why are you so quiet?" he asked. "By the way, do you know why I called you here?"

"No, I don't" I answered. "I don't know why I am here."

"I know you are one of the bright students here," he complimented. "And it is my duty to encourage you. That is one of the reasons I called you here. Moreover, I like coffee a lot, and I want you to make me coffee sometimes."

My heart nearly jumped out of my chest. I knew that he was setting a trap.

"But, I …," I wanted to protest, but he didn't let me finish.

"Don't worry. You go now and come back here tomorrow after school," he said.

I answered him, a little bit bolder than before. "Tomorrow, I have to get ready for my exam. I have an exam the day after."

"Little lady, do what I said. Come back tomorrow!" Angrily, he stood up and went outside, leaving me behind.

I could control my tears no more. They flowed down my cheeks.

When I got back, my friend saw that my eyes were red with tears and was shocked.

"What did he tell you, you look terrible?" she quizzed me. "Did he discover that you are a Christian?"

"No, he wants me to come to his house and make him coffee," I told her. "By the way, I saw your relative in his house."

She didn't let me finish.

"In the name of Jesus!" she loudly declared. Then she continued, "My sister, don't lose heart. We will pray, and God will give you courage."

She then told me how they pressured her relative, entrapped her, and made her a slave to satisfy their sexual desires.

"Do you know? He told me to come to his house and make him coffee tomorrow." I told her sobbing. My friend had no answer and didn't know what to say.

"Whatever happens, don't go," she advised. "Moreover, God doesn't let us be tested beyond our capacity. He will provide a way."

Her words filled my heart with boldness.

The next day, the hour of my appointment arrived. I knew the consequences if I didn't go to his house at the appointed time. Whatever happened, like Moses I decided to bear suffering for the sake of Christ and stay undefiled.

The next day during the morning line up, I heard my name called. Trembling, I went to my commander who had called my name.

"You! Why didn't you show up at the appointment you had with Colonel Tecle?" he asked me. Without waiting for my response, he ordered, "Now, go."

"Where?" I asked. "I have to go to class; I have an exam."

"You heard me! Go!" he replied, pointing to the open field under the brutal Sawa sun where students were often punished. "From now onward, you sit here till noon."

I sat down in the dirt under the scorching sun. The sun beat on me till I had a headache.

At around 12:30, my commander came and told me, "Stand up! Hurry up!" and took me to the Colonel's house.

On the way to the Colonel's house he said with disgust, "You slut, have you forgotten what benefits you would get if you made the colonel coffee?" I didn't respond. When we arrived, he took me inside and went back to his place.

The colonel scowled and asked me, "Why didn't you come yesterday?"

"I had an exam, and I had to prepare," I replied.

"So did you take your exam?" he asked in a derisive tone.

I started sobbing and replied, "No, I didn't. I was punished."

"If you do not obey orders, let alone missing exams, you will even be expelled from the school. Now, you go and come back tomorrow at 1 pm," he said.

"O God!" I complained silently. "After enduring the harsh punishment, it isn't over yet, and I have to come tomorrow?"

4

School with a Divided Heart

Thinking about my appointment with the Colonel, I went to class. First thing, my teacher summoned me.

"Why didn't you take the exam yesterday? Were you sick?" he asked.

I wept silently. "Don't weep? Have you missed your family?" he inquired. And a moment later, he asked me again, "Are you ok?"

I told him what happened. I saw his face go dark. He had a sigh of sadness. "They are gambling with our sisters' and our lives," he bitterly complained, grumbling. He looked sideways and said, "These are monsters. Their intention is not for us to teach and for you to study." He then added some words of encouragement, "Don't be discouraged. And may God help you. Don't you worry, I will let you take the exam next week. Don't weep. May your enemies weep."

My mind was divided until the end of the school day between the question whether to go or not to go. I had my lunch and offered a prayer to my Savior and then went to the place of my appointment.

The colonel's house was open, and I went closer to it.

"Good afternoon," I said s I came closer to the door. The young woman I saw in the house the other day answered me.

"Have you had a good afternoon, Aster?" she asked me calling me by my name. She asked me to take a seat.

"The colonel had asked me to come. Isn't he at home?" I asked.

"No, he is not. But he has asked me to tell you to wait for him," she told me. "He will be back in about half an hour."

I thought half an hour was like an eternity. "What would you like to have? Anything to drink or eat? The colonel's house has everything," she said and smiled at me.

"No thank you, I have already had my lunch," I answered. She sat beside me. The room became quiet for a few minutes. She then started talking to me. I told her that her relative [mentioning her name] was my friend.

She bowed her head and asked, "So you know her? She must have told you everything." Tears began to roll down her face. I wept with her.

"Don't lose heart. God is alive," I tried to comfort her. "The only thing we should do is trust in Him."

"This colonel who has called you," she started, "is a friend of the man who coerced me into a love relationship with him. The suffering and troubles I have borne are too much to share with anyone. You see, I cannot concentrate on my studies. Instead, I have become a slave, a woman to make them their coffee and satistfy their desires. I have become a useless woman. Look! You listen. Take care! Don't give in to these monsters! It is much better if you escape this country."

I knew that she must have been very bitter. In my heart, I resolved, "I will pay any price so that I don't fall into their hands."

Before we finished talking, the colonel arrived.

"Good girl, so today you have come to make coffee for me?"

I never had such a surge of boldness in my life before.

"Colonel," I told him, "I am here to keep the appointment, not to make coffee. After all, my parents sent me here to study. They didn't send me to make coffee."

The colonel was very furious.

"I don't think you know any respect," he said. "So you have come to disrespect me this much! My intention was to support your educational efforts because I know you are a bright student. But I have never seen such arrogance! Now, get out of my sight!"

He chased me out of his house. For this reason, I was punished for a week mercilessly. For a week, I had to bear the heat of the blazing sun. I thought the seven days were like seven years. The situation was so bad that I yearned for the time I would see my home.

Many young men and women began to miss classes. Many of them escaped from the camp and attempted to cross the border to the Sudan or other neighbouring countries. Those that were caught were thrown into jail.

As the Tigrigna saying goes, "A day and a dog come unbidden." The day we had to sit for matriculation exams arrived. Due to the punishment I endured throughout, I had suffered a lot, and this had jeopardized my preparation to some extent. However, God was with me and helped me study for my exams sufficiently. Soon, the exams were over, and we started packing.

One evening before we left the camp, my friend, three believers, and I were in a secret Bible study and prayer meeting. We were the only participants. The atmosphere was wonderful. We began to thank God, for we saw that He had supported us through tough times, which we endured.

We were in such a wonderful mood when suddenly a voice ordered us, "Stand up where you are!"

It was a military order. We glanced to our right and our left, and we saw three soldiers standing as pillars.

Foretaste of the Suffering to Come

Peace settled in the place for a few minutes. To be honest, we were a little afraid. One of the soldiers thundered at us: "You stupid girls! What are you doing here in the dark? Crouch!"

"What is in their hands?" the second soldier asked.

The man who raged against us struck my back with his stick. Loudly, he quizzed us, "What are you doing here?"

I answered him, unconscious of my words, "We are praying."

I saw his face turn red.

"Praying? I see. You are *pente*! You traitors! You CIA agents!"

He tried to intimidate us. He told his comrade to search us. The other man searched us from the crown of our heads to the soles of our feet. From my bag, he found the fragmented Bible, which I had compiled by pulling out some chapters and books from the original Bible for sharing with friends.

Half an hour later, they took us and threw us in a room.

We prayed the whole night. We prayed that God would abundantly give us His grace in the time of our suffering and troubles.

It was about time to go back to join our families. Instead, we had been arrested. We felt Satan whispering into the heart of each of us, "You won't see your families!" Especially, one of us was very troubled.

The next morning, the same soldiers who found us the night before came and took us away. They made us stand in the presence of Colonel Tecle, the same person who had given me a lot of trouble before.

When he saw me, Colonel Tecle said mockingly, "You trash! So you are one of the defilers of our society! You are good for nothing!" He showered me with a lot of abusive words.

"Are you a *pente*?" he asked me again. "I am asking you! Answer me!" He tried to intimidate me.

"I am a Christian. I am a follower of Christ!" I answered him boldly.

"You are a bold one!" he sarcastically remarked. "This is a camp, not a religious institution. And don't you know that your 'faith' is the enemy of the nation?"

I was filled with more boldness. "I have done nothing wrong up to this minute," I answered him. "It is my right to practice my faith the way I see fit." I realized that the Spirit of God who was on Stephen had filled me with boldness.

"Take her away from my presence!" the Colonel ordered in a rage. "Please, take them away and punish them, as harshly as you can!" he gave them a stern order. "Then, we will see if Jesus will rescue them!"

They took us all away. They ordered us to pour water from a barrel onto the ground. Then, they ordered us to roll in the mud. We were unable to disobey the order so we rolled in the mud until our bodies began to bleed. We were completely muddied.

We had eaten nothing since early in the morning. We almost fainted due to the hunger and the intense heat. We felt that the tears that rolled to the ground made it even more muddied. Caked in mud, we stayed in the open area until sunset.

At nightfall, we were ordered to wash and change our clothes. We asked if we could go and collect our clothes since our clothes were not with us. They, however, had already brought our stuff.

After we washed and ate, we felt our souls being revived. We were closely guarded by the soldiers nearby so we could not talk to one another. In our hearts, though, we asked God to protect us and grant us grace.

Without being conscious of our surroundings and the passage of time, dawn came. However, we were unable to stand up as we had become weak-kneed. Our backs were especially hurting and because we had been rolling on the ground they wouldn't straighten. We were ordered to follow the soldiers to the punishment fields again. There was nothing we could do, so we went with them, compelled by a military order.

The soldiers punished us very severely. At 1 pm, the time the sun shines most intensely down on Sawa, we were told to carry a bucket full of sand and move in circles. We almost fainted due to the punishment. Rolling in the mud, military punishment, and carrying a bucket full of sand and moving in circles in the blazing sun became our daily routine. I am sure some of you will find this story unbelievable.

One day, due to the excessive punishment, one of the sisters fainted, and she was taken to the hospital. As for me, I endured the punishment for one month. As I rolled on the mud, I felt my strength leave me. I could not stand straight and had to lie there exhausted. Finally, I also fainted.

6

Til the End

Three hours later, I found myself in a locked room. In a weak voice, I called the names of the sisters suffering with me and said in delirium, "Where am I? And who brought me here? Am I still being punished? Have we finished our studies?"

My friend Rahwa said "Call on the name of Jesus. Rest a little." She touched my head and began praying for me. After I slept for two hours, my strength returned miraculously and I began to call Rahwa's name. She rose and gave me some food, which she had put aside for me. After I had eaten a little, I asked her what had happened the day before.

"Yesterday, there was intense heat. Your strength failed you, and you fainted. And I screamed. So the soldier struck me with the butt of his gun. I was afraid, so I stood a little distance away from you. Some of them said, 'Let's take her to the hospital, she may die in our hand.' Then I heard the commander say, 'Be quiet! Just pour some water on her. She doesn't need any medical attention.' Later, they poured cold water on you. They told us to carry you away so we carried you on our backs and brought you here."

I wept and thanked God for giving me the opportunity to live.

I told her, "When I was asleep, I heard a voice saying 'Take heart! Take heart! I am with you til the end of the age. Be faithful until death. Don't bow to their statue. Our light and momentary troubles are achieving for us an eternal glory.'"

Many verses ran through my mind so I told Rahwa, "Take courage, God is with us." In turn, I began to encourage her. In amazement, she confirmed, "Even in my heart I received the same message during the night."

We held hands and asked God for grace for the rest of the difficult days ahead. The door was struck, the customary military order was given, and we prepared to go to our usual punishment.

"Be quick! Pack your clothes quick!" an order was given to us.

Having packed our clothes, we fell in line. Then they took us to the worst prison in Sawa.

Truly, it was a very terrible prison. We found any girls in the prison. None of them had any semblance of beauty. All had become ashen. Distress and suffering were clearly seen on their faces.

We stayed for about three months in that terrible prison. It was heartbreaking to hear the stories of some of the girls. One of the girls was caught crossing the border. She, her two friends, and three other young men paid the smugglers to lead them from Sawa to the Sudan. They started their journey, but when they reached the border, the smugglers abandoned them. The young woman and her friends walked a long distance since they didn't know the direction they should have followed. They became very exhausted. One of the young women became very ill, and shortly after, she breathed her last in the desert. They didn't know what to do. They put a sign over the body of their dead companion and continued walking aimlessly for a long distance.

As they were walking, suddenly they heard a voice that ordered them to stop. Terrified, they began to run. A round of shots began to whistle around them. Immediately, two of the young men and the remaining young woman were hit by bullets.

"Then," the young woman told me, "I fainted. After I regained consciousness, they brought me to this prison."

The many stories of the prisoners were devastating to hear. Not a few women developed harmful addictions due to the suffering and trouble they endured in the prison.

Already, matriculation (matric for short) results had been announced. I had no doubt that I would get a perfect score. However, it was very hard to get information about my score while still in prison. I still had no information one month after the announcement.

One day, a Christian brother I knew who used to work in the prison brought us clothes, soap, *tihni*, and other necessities. I had no idea who told him that we were in the prison. I was unable to ask him many questions. Since the situation in the prison left people terrified, no one could speak about one's true feelings.

"Can you, please, check about my matric score and bring me word?" I asked him.

"I will try," he answered. "By the way, your friend has sent you a letter," he said.

He took out a letter very carefully. He secretly handed me the letter and immediately left. I was anxious to read the letter. However, I was afraid that the guards might spot me reading it. Therefore, I patiently waited until nightfall.

When I got the opportunity, I took out the piece of paper, opened it, and began reading it. In the letter, I found sad and happy news. The letter had news about my family's knowledge of my imprisonment and that they were worried about me. In addition, it had information that my friends and I had gotten perfect scores. I told my prison mates what had happened. To be honest, because we got passing scores, we felt that they would release us.

A week later, my name and the names of my friends were called. "Pack very quickly!" we were ordered. We were overjoyed. I was filled with joy because I had a dream to be a doctor, and I assumed I was going to medical school. They put us in a bus, and our journey started.

7

To the Place that Spits Fire

After a long journey, we knew we had arrived in Asmara. I felt my heart filled with joy. My sisters and I knew very well that the few months of suffering and trouble were terrible. Unusually, Asmara was in deep darkness and silence.

"Are they going to leave us here, in the bus station in the dark and tell us to go to our houses by ourselves?" I thought. The bus stopped at one spot.

One soldier ordered us, "Get your clothes and get off!"

Everyone got off one after another. The soldiers led us towards a building.

"Why are they still holding us? Why don't they let us go home?" I complained silently in my heart.

There were about thirty of us. After we had taken our seats, they brought us dinner, and we sat to eat. Due to the long journey and anxious thoughts, we were unable to eat properly.

"Will they tell us to go home or will they keep us here for the night?" This question tugged at my heart. Everyone was very tired. So, everyone fell asleep in the seat that was given.

I was exhausted. However, I was unable to sleep. At about 1 am, a rough voice ordered us, "Wake up and line up, everyone!" Every one of us lined up according to the instruction. They led us to a bus and ordered us to board.

"They can't take us home in the dead of night!" I thought to myself.

My prison mate and friend sat beside me. "I don't think they will let us go. I don't have that kind of good feeling," she told me.

I didn't agree with her opinion so I said, "In the Name of Jesus, don't say such things! God has brought our suffering to an end!"

My friend replied "Aster, it is good to be ready for all kinds of eventualities! We should be faithful to God at all times and all places! Therefore, if they let us go home, good! If something different happens, it is good to remember that God has purposes."

Her words pierced my heart, and I told her, "You are absolutely right!" We agreed to pray and ask God to give us grace abundantly.

The bus started its journey. We realized that we had left Asmara behind. To be honest, I had a very strong desire to go home. I felt very bad and sobbed for almost half an hour. In the middle of such a mood, a loud voice echoed in my ears, "Blessed are those who grieve, for they will be comforted."

My heart was strengthened. I felt God's grace pour abundantly on me. I felt I was like the Apostle Peter. In prison, he was surrounded by a multitude of soldiers and was shortly to be taken to his death. However, he soundly slept. I had a similar experience – I had a peaceful and pleasant sleep. At 7 am, my friend shook me awake.

"Aster, we are on the Massawa road," she told me.

I was confused. "Massawa? Massawa road?"

She was right. We were travelling on the Massawa – Gahtelay road. I immediately realized that they were taking us to Wia.

My sister had told me that Wia was a very terrible place. A number of people were incarcerated in Wia. I told my friend that they were taking us to Wia. I comforted her by saying that God had helped us in the past and could be depended on in the future.

I began to tell her a story my sister had told me about a Christian brother.

"This brother was under punishment because he had a Bible while he was in the National Service. After the punishment, his commander called him to his office and ordered him not to read the Bible and pray. However, the brother did not stop reading the Bible. His commander called him to his office again.

"'Will you abandon the faith you are following or not?'" he threatened him.

"The brother answered him, 'I will not.' The commander ordered his soldiers to tie him in a style nicknamed 'Helicopter.' They tied his hands and feet behind his back. They poured dirty water on his head and threw him on the ground under the hot sun for long hours. The brother suffered tremendously. This type of punishment became his daily routine.

"One day, the commander called him. 'How about now? Will you abandon your faith?' he thundered at him."

"The brother answered him, 'What worse punishment can I suffer? Therefore, I won't deny the Lord Jesus. Not today, not in the future!'"

"After this, they put him in a dark place for a long time. One day, deliberately, they took him out of the hole at broad daylight. His eyes were permanetly damaged by the bright light, and he was blinded. He begged to see a doctor. They repeatedly answered him, 'If you want to get medical help, first deny your faith.' And they deprived him of medical attention he badly needed."

"This brother stood steadfast in the faith in the face of suffering and trouble. One day, they brought him to Wia, the place to which we are headed. They locked him in a tin-house. Wia is a horrible place. Let alone human beings, you don't wish even animals to live there. After suffering for an extended time, this brother passed away in martyrdom."

Tears rolled down my friend's cheeks and flooded her face.

My friend asked me, "Do you think we will be able to bear all this suffering?"

"God knows." I tried to comfort her. After a long journey, we arrived at Wia, known as the place that spits fire.

In Wia

A military barracks set in a deep valley, Wia is forty five kilometres south of Massawa on the road to Assab. Wia is a very dreadful place. The heat is unbearable with tempratures soaring to 120F. It appears as if the sun has physically come down. Everyone's face was covered with grief and sadness. The bitterness and pain in people's hearts was not hard to see. Everyone walked with his or her head down. Death and the angel of darkness had overshadowed it.

They put my friends and me in an underground room. I don't think you can realize how hard it is to be incarcerated in an underground room in such a hot place. We felt as if our bodies were boiling in a blazing fire. We prayed in earnest so that the God of Meshach, Shadrach, and Abed-Nego would live among us. The young women we found in the room gave us *tihni* to drink. However, they didn't have any food. Therefore, we as the new arrivals went to bed with empty stomachs in the locked room.

I felt so sad and woke up. "O God, why do you allow such trouble in my life at such a tender age?"

But, the story of Paul and Silas came to my heart immediately. As Paul and Silas thanked God in chains, I also needed to thank God. Therefore, I loudly began to thank Him.

"O God, I thank you for you have counted me worthy to suffer for your Name." Then, I began to shout, calling on the name of Jesus, "Jesus … Jesus."

My companions felt that I had lost my mind because of the excessive heat. So they shut my mouth and began pouring water on my head. I slept in the arms of my companions because I was very exhausted.

At six in the morning, the whistle blew. All of us went out of our room. The sun in Wia arose before people woke up from their sleep. We were told to walk, collect stones, and pile the stones in one area. We worked for long hours and piled the stones in one spot. In addition, we were told to gather gravel and cover the ground with it. This became our daily routine.

One morning, we woke up and started to collect stones as usual. After we collected some stones, I was unable to bear the heat. I tried my best to endure. However, half-way through the day I fell flat on my face and fainted.

My companions speedily began pouring water on me, as they told me later. Some others mixed *tihni* and had me drink it. A few hours later, I recovered.

One of the sisters said, "Aster, you are really very fortunate. You should praise God. About a month ago, a sister collapsed as we collected stones. To help her, we poured water on her. However, one of the commanders thundered and threatened us, 'Mind your business! You will suffer the same fate!' We backed off and did nothing."

"One of us boldly asked the commander if she could help her. He refused to listen to her. He answered her and mocked us, 'Use the tricks of the Asmarinos with other people, not me.'"

"An hour later, a soldier came and talked to him. Only then did he allow us. However, our sister was already beyond help. She had already died. We shook the place with our screams. For that reason, we were locked underground for two weeks."

She told me this in tears, filled with bitterness. I was in the middle of a circle of young women. A soldier suddenly appeared and shouted at us, "You cheats, what are you doing here? Go and get busy," and he began striking us with his big stick.

One of the sisters boldly told him what happened.

"So what?" he retorted. "Go at once!" he ordered us angrily. My legs were very weak, I began to collect pieces of rock and stones. We continued this way for six months.

For the first few months there, I received no information about my family. I didn't know if, on their part, they had any information about my whereabouts. I missed them very terribly, and this became a worse challenge than the place in which I was imprisoned. To be honest, due to the excessive suffering and trouble, I could see no bright future. I began sobbing alone. During such a time, some verses came into my heart: "God enlightens my darkness." "He rescued me for He loved me." "I scale fences in Your Name." "We are more than conquerors." I received these and some others. These verses supported my heart, and, in the middle of the extreme suffering, I began to be joyful because of the presence of the blessed Holy Spirit.

One day, we sat at the table for a meal after we returned from collecting stones. I never ate before saying grace. So to start eating, I bowed my head in prayer.

Suddenly, a soldier shouted at me, “You son of a b –! Stand up!”

He struck me on my head with the stick in his hand. There was a rock near me. I fell on the rock and lay on the ground. My body and my clothes were bloodied. I also felt my hand had become dislocated. They carried me to the clinic. I was unable to bear the pain from my head and my hand. Because of the intense pain, I lost consciousness.

9

Sustained by God's Grace

A life God has willed to preserve does not die before its time. After three days, I found my head bandaged and my hand in a cast. I felt as if my head was a separate entity and didn't belong to the rest of my body.

A young man who stood near me said, "Good morning. Don't lose heart. Your injury is not that bad. You will be ok." I had a lot of pain so I struggled just to say a few words, "Can you please give me a painkiller?"

The young man frowned and went out without answering me. I thought that he had gone out to bring me a painkiller. However, my hopes were dashed. The young man failed to come back, and I went to bed in pain. In the middle of the pain and in and out of sleep, a song filled my heart: "God has a plan even through this experience; God has a plan through these circumstances; It is to beautify Him and show His mercy and love!"

The song began to ring as a big bell in my spirit. In the midst of all the suffering and pain, my spirit began to rejoice like a child. I felt as if I had entered another world.

While I was in this mood, the medical officer I had asked for a painkiller shook me and I woke up. "You must have been in a very deep sleep? Has the pain subsided? Take these tablets."

I reluctantly woke up.

"Why did you wake me up?" I angrily asked him. He just bowed his head and didn't answer me. He realized that I had become very angry.

"I am sorry. I was trying to help," he said. "When you asked me for painkillers, I did my best and brought you these because you don't find painkillers here. I know I shouldn't have woken you up. You see, I woke you up thinking the tablets would relieve your pain."

I felt a little ashamed of myself. "You are right. I was in another world," I began to explain. "And I didn't want to leave that world. That's why."

He took my cue and said, "Another world? Is it a world that snatches people out of their anxiety and suffering? Or another?" He smiled at me.

To be honest, since I was in pain, I really wanted him to give me the tablets and leave. However, I didn't want the opportunity that presented itself to vanish. I didn't want to miss telling him of the Gospel of Jesus, my Saviour who loved me, and gave me life and had ordered me to tell others of the good news.

Therefore, I smiled and told him, "Yes, there is a world more pleasant than this."

He immediately said, "To be honest, it is good to leave this hell, even if it is only in one's dreams."

"Do you know what the Bible says?" I asked him. I was about to start talking when he said, "Please, don't continue. We could get arrested for this." I could see he was shaking from fear.

"Don't you worry," I told him. I told him about the Lord for about ten minutes. He gave me the tablets and told me, "I will come back tomorrow."

He left immediately.

The next morning, one of the camp officers came and told me, "Is this better than what you rejected? If you don't change your ways, you will lose your life."

I answered him boldly, "My life is from God. What power does man have?"

"I am amazed by the spirit of the *pente*?" he wondered, "If power were God's, would you be here?"

I don't know where my boldness came from but confidently, I responded,"My God is in Heaven. And he does whatever He wills."

He retorted back and mocked me, "Then, let Him save you from here!"

"Our sufferings, which are temporary, bring us eternal glory," I answered him.

"What misfortune is this?" He threatened me, enraged by my answer. "Get better a little. You will see me then."

In the afternoon, the medical officer who evaluated me came, accompanied by another man.

"Here are your tablets," he told me, "Meet this man. He is like you." He then left me with the newcomer.

The newcomer, a Christian brother named Simon, began to ask me about my condition seriously. I had no energy to tell him all about myself. Due to my pain, I was unable to speak to him.

"Do you work here?" I asked Simon, smiling.

"What work is here?" he asked. "There is only punishment."

"How long have you been here?" I asked again. "Are you a member of the National Service?"

"Next month, it will be my fifth year!"

"Five years?"

"This is easy," Simon told me calmly. "But with the Lord everything is good." My face flooded with tears.

He comforted me, "Don't weep! Why, if only we are fit enough to bear suffering for the Lord!"

"How did you come here?" I asked him earnestly.

"It is a long story."

He began telling me his story, "You would be surprised. One evening, I was in a prayer meeting in Asmara. For a long time, we prayed and studied the Bible. We had a wonderful time as the Spirit of God was with us."

I forgot about my illness for the time being.

"What happened next? Tell me before the soldiers come!" I asked, interrupting him.

"Then, a young man approached a Christian from my

neighbourhood, who prayed and studied the Bible with us. The young man told the Christian, 'I want to learn the Bible. Please, give me a Bible.'"

"You know the joy you feel when a non-believer asks you to learn the Bible. The Christian started teaching the Bible to the young man. After some weeks, he brought him to the place where we held our Christian meetings. The young man joined us and studied the Bible and prayed with us for one month."

"One day, while we were in the meeting, some policemen the young man had led there, surrounded the house we were in. Then, the policemen treated us roughly and took us to the Fifth Police Station. Then, …"

Before he finished his story, the man who brought him to me came and told him, panting, "Hurry up! They are here. Escape this way."

Simon told me, "I will come back another day," and he left before finishing his testimony.

10

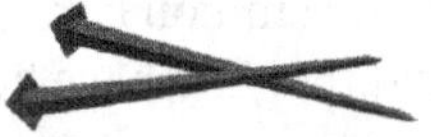

God's Help

Three weeks had gone by since I arrived at the clinic. There was no medical help except painkillers. A young woman who slept in another bed beside me was shivering because of malaria. She was unable to bear the sickness, and she screamed in a delirium. I realized that she had ague.

I fought back my pain and started praying for her. A number of people were in the clinic, and the camp guards kept watch on us. With the physical pain and constant watch of the guards, it was hard to have a heart-to-heart talk even when we went out for a toilet break.

One afternoon, the sister beside me was in great pain and talked in delirium. I could bear her pain no more. Her pain (added to mine) troubled me. I do not know how I stood up. I went to the young woman and prayed for her, putting my hand on her and weeping profusely.

"Oh God, who will help if you don't in this weary and dry

place of suffering, where people's tears are not heard and their cries are ignored, where the violent and torturers are many? As your servant David said, 'I lift my eyes to mountains. Where does my help come from? My help comes from the One who created the Heavens and the Earth.' This sister's help is from you. Therefore, I pray in the name of Your Son, Jesus Christ, to lay Your good and helpful Hand on her. I thank you because I believe in Your word and that You have healed her."

I prayed in tears and weeping. The amazing thing was as I prayed, the sister slept calmly as if she were a baby that had been rocked. I thanked my God and went back to my bed.

The difference between the young woman's bed and mine wasn't longer than three metres (about 9 ft). However, I thought it was three kilometres on my way back to my bed. I was unable to walk. In my heart, I was worried that the guard may come and find me. I stood like a statue. I felt my head was like a heavy stone. I was unable to bear the pain of my hand. In my heart, I began to call on the name of Jesus. What I feared happened just then.

One of the guards came running and thundered at me, "Where have you been?"

Fearfully, I told him, "I was in the toilet room."

"Is the toilet room this way? Go! Go to your bed!" he told me. I struggled to my bed and suffered from my pain the whole night.

The next morning, I asked the medical officer who gave me painkillers to bring me some more.

He told me, "Sister, I don't think I can get you any painkillers today."

"Why?" I asked him.

"Yesterday, a guard saw you as you prayed for the young woman," he told me. "He watched everything you did. Then, he asked you what you were doing. For this reason, we are instructed not to give you any medicine."

To be honest, it was very hard to bear to get such an inhumane answer when you are in terrible pain. However, I was sure that I would be able to accept it because of the God who gave me His grace abundantly.

After we had some crumbs of bread and our cup of tea, the commander came seeking trouble.

"You," he addressed me. "I am talking to you! Are you going to stop your activities or not? I want a direct answer."

"I am recovering in this health facility. I have done nothing wrong," I told him.

His face turned red with rage. "Who has appointed you to pray for people here? Who has appointed you a priest?"

I interrupted him. "I don't think prayer is wrong. Our fathers and mothers taught us to pray."

"Shut up! You traitor," he shouted at me. He then softened his tone and said, "If you sign this paper which states that you have revoked your faith, I will send you to Asmara to get medical treatment at Halibet Hospital or Enda Korea." [These are two general hospitals in the capital]

I don't know why I smiled but I did. "My faith is mine. My faith has not become a problem for me. Why should I revoke my faith?"

"So you choose suffering?" he asked. "If that is your choice, that is fine with me."

He then became angry and asked me, "By the way, who converted you into this faith? Do any of your family members follow it?"

I didn't answer him as if I hadn't heard. He was enraged.

"You will see our stick is not weak. We will beat you into perfect subjection! You will start blabbering whether you like it or not." He yelled "Crazy!" to me and left the room.

One of the things that amazed me was that I was not scared at all. It must be for this reason that the Lord said, "Don't be afraid of those who kill only the flesh but Him who can kill both flesh and the spirit." The apostle Paul was right to boast, "Who shall separate us from love of the Lord?"

At about six or seven o'clock in the evening, the young woman I had prayed for came to me. I was afraid in case I might have another problem on her account. After she greeted me, she said, "Thank you! Thank you!" and she began to weep.

"Please, be a little quiet! They will hear us talking!" I tried to calm her.

"Let them!" she told me. "What worse thing can we receive? Death is a good thing. If we are dead, we would be spared from such suffering."

She was very bitter.

"Don't be discouraged" I told her. "Dawn and light follow pitch darkness. And this too will pass," and I comforted her.

The woman told me, "You see, I had to endure this terrible

malaria for one month! However, when you laid your hand me on and prayed for me, I felt something very hot. In my life, I never had such a peaceful sleep. Now, I have no pain, nor do I experience delirium. Truly, God is with you!"

I thanked God very much. I praised Him because He was, He is and He will be forever, and I put my trust in Him. I told the sister the word of God, and I boldly prayed for her.

I then asked her how she came to be in Wia. She told me that they brought her from Massawa for commiting harlotry. She told me, "Life became very unbearable. And our husbands and fathers left [for National Service]. So our children had nothing to eat. We started doing things we didn't want to, selling our bodies. There was no choice. What choice did we have?"

She wept bitterly.

I felt my heart break. "O God, when will you come back for us?" I wept with her. After the woman went to her bed, I lay down on my bed to pray. However, I felt a terrible pain in my head. I think it was due to the weeping. The pulsating headache felt like a repeated strike on my skull. I could not bear the pain. I groaned in my heart and prayed, "O God, please heal me!" The painkiller they gave me was now no more.

After a difficult night, morning finally arrived.

11

By Faith

After sometime, as usual, the soldier who brought us food came with breakfast. I had no appetite because I still felt the pain from the night before. So I asked him, "I would really like to have a painkiller instead of this breakfast! Please!" I begged him.

"I don't know about these things!" he murmured, leaving my breakfast on the table. Even though I was very hungry, I could not eat the breakfast.

I had suffered the whole night from the severe pain. At dawn, I felt better and slept a little. However, I slept for only an hour. A very loud voice, which was too loud and made my ears hurt, woke me up. I was in a very deep sleep, and I felt it was a dream. I had a very hard time opening my eyes. When I heard the instruction to wake up, I sat up on my bed, though it was a struggle. And before me I saw the commander that always threatened me.

Enraged, he asked me, "Why don't you give me peace? Has anyone appointed you a preacher here? Why are you doing this? Is it because you think we can't do anything?"

He tried to intimidate me. I realized that the chat I had with the woman yesterday had enraged him. He then ordered the two soldiers who came with him, "Take her away!"

They took me outside and ordered me to lie outside under the hot sun. The blazing sun worsened my pain in the extreme. To be honest, this was too much to bear, and I prayed to God to take me home to Him.

At dusk, a soldier came and took me back to the health facility. I decided to eat the little they gave me. However, no sleep came all that night.

Then, I saw the commander rushing toward me. I could see from the way he walked that he was very angry.

"Now, what do they have against me? And what are they going to say?" I thought. In no time, he stood before me like a statue.

With uncharacteristic behavior, he wished me good morning and asked me how I was that morning. I immediately knew that he was laying a trap for me. I knew in my spirit that the warm greeting masked some evil thought.

I answered his greeting with, "Praise God, I am fine." I could see how the word 'God' caused him so much discomfort and how it stole his peace.

He calmly said, "Your health is not in excellent condition at this time. You have the right to get good medical care. Our plan is to send you to Asmara. However, we request that you meet one condition. And that is to sign this paper."

He put the paper on my bed and ordered the soldier who came with him, “Help her to sit down and give her a pen!”

I told him, “If you want me to sign, I must first read and understand what I sign. Otherwise, how can I sign something I don’t know and didn’t read?”

I saw his face go dark. It must have been to hide his evil intentions that he wore a happy face for just a few minutes. He became like a tiger in the flash of a moment.

“You are disgraceful!” he shouted at me. “You don’t know what respect is! Did you suspect we would let you sign something mysterious? Or something deadly? Look, you have this opportunity until tomorrow. You sign this paper whether you have read it or not. If you refuse, you will face the worst!”

He left in a hurry, filled with anger.

I began to read the paper. It stated that I was a criminal and I was a traitor to the government and the people, and that I had worked against my country. It also stated that I realized and admitted my mistake, and I was requesting forgiveness. It went on to say that from that day onwards, I would not dabble in any religious activities, not go to any religious meetings, and would not get involved in any Christian activities.

When I read the word ‘traitor,’ a verse from Hebrews rang in my heart: “By faith Moses, when he had grown up, refused to be known as the son of Pharaoh’s daughter. He chose to be mistreated along with the people of God rather than to enjoy the pleasures of sin for a short time. He regarded disgrace for the sake of Christ as of greater value than the treasures of Egypt, because he was looking ahead to his reward. By faith he left Egypt, not fearing the king’s anger; he persevered because he saw him who is invisible.”

I promised that I would never deny my God. I left the paper unsigned on the small table nearby.

12

If You don't Sign

It was amazing. The young man who brought us food was late, and we didn't have any breakfast. It was almost noon. Hungry and tired, I laid down on my bed. Two hours later, someone shook me, and I woke up. It was the young man, Simon, who didn't finish relating his story. He came with the medical officer.

"Good afternoon. Why did you have a long sleep? Aren't you ok?" the medical officer asked me.

"I am ok. But, to be honest, I am hungry. I didn't have even a bite since day break."

He was filled with compassion. I saw that his eyes were watering.

"They use even food as a weapon of punishment," he murmured. "Hunger in such a hot place, it is terrible. Don't worry. Give me a minute. I will bring you lunch."

He went out. Half an hour later, he came back carrying lunch, tea, bread, *tihni*, and juice. I was overjoyed. However, I was worried that they would catch us red-handed. I ate until I had enough.

"Put away the leftovers here. If they gave you dinner later, fine. If not, you can have this."

"What is this paper?" he asked me. I gave it to him to read. "Read it!"

"What is there to read? Haven't they worn us out with this paper?" he asked and added, "What is your decision?"

I told him. "In the name of Jesus, I won't sign it."

"The Lord bless you! We will pray so that God will give you power."

"God bless you," I told him. "Now, I want to hear the rest of your testimony."

"Where did I stop?" he asked me.

"You told me that they took you to the Fifth Police Station from the house of the prayer meeting," I told him.

Simon continued his story. "At the Fifth Police Station, they put all the females in one place and the males in another. For one month, they left us alone. However, praise be to God, beyond our expectations, we enjoyed fellowship through Bible lessons and prayer meetings there."

"After one month, the police station called some men. I was among them. They locked me up in a very dark cell, in a villa. For one whole week, I saw no one. After that, someone started to question me seriously. I think he was from the security services."

"He asked me these and other questions: 'Who is funding you? Where is the money that you received?'"

"I told him that nobody funded us, and that I was a follower of God. The next day, two strong men in plain clothes came and beat me until I was bloodied all over. They tried very hard to make me tell them things."

"I didn't say a word except 'God bless you.' They locked me up in that room, and I didn't leave the place for about three months. I knew that my other friends had the same fate."

"After that, they took me out of the room and sent me to the prison in Adi Abeito."

Adi Abeito was the main prison for Asmara [the capital] and the surrounding areas. Shipping containers as well as prison cells were used as detention and punishment facilities there.

"The prison was terrible, and I stayed there for seven months living on dry bread," he continued.

"After that, they gave me a piece of paper like the one they have given you and told me to sign it. I didn't sign because I could not do it with a clear conscience. After that, they took me to a place called Mai Sirwa [another prison in the network of prisons around Asmara]. I was locked there in a shipping container for many months."

"One day, one of the young men locked up in the container got very ill. He was about to faint. It was against the rules to open the window of the container by ourselves. When I saw that the young man was very ill, I kicked the window open. The young man, when he got some fresh air, started to recover."

“Later, the guards came and asked, ‘Who opened the window?’ They pressed us to give them the name of the person who opened the window.”

“Together, we told them about the illness of our friend, but they didn’t care. They warned us sternly, ‘If you don’t tell us the name of the person who opened the window, you will suffer severe additional punishment.’ My cell-mates didn’t want to speak. I told the guards that it was me because I didn’t want them to suffer on my account.”

“It is a miracle that a human being can survive such a beating. They beat me up until I fainted. And they left me like people do a dead person. However, I am still alive probably because God wanted me to tell of His glory.”

“After a one year stay in Mai Sirwa, they brought me here, to Wia. This is my fifth year here.”

He told me a little out of his long testimony. “I must go now before they come back. Night is falling. I will come on another day, and I will talk to you. Stay strong and stay in the faith.”

I fervently prayed so that, if it was His will, the sufferings my brothers and I endured would end. The next morning, the commander, as usual, came seeking to cause trouble.

“Where is the paper? Give it to me,” He said. I gave it to him.

“Why didn’t you sign it?”

“I don’t want to sign it,” I told him. “I don’t think it is right to sign it.”

“Bide your time,” he threatened me, “I will show you who I am.”

Loudly, he ordered the soldiers, "Take her to that place!" He shouted at them. They took me away, but I didn't know where they were taking me.

The soldiers started on the trip to the place they knew, according to the commander's instruction. Because of the blazing sun and the heat, I thought the half hour trip felt like a thirty year journey. Half way, I begged them for a break. However, they didn't listen to me and didn't allow me to rest. After a short while, my head became dizzy, and I collapsed. The soldiers lifted me up and gave me some water and *tihni.* I felt better, got strengthened, and continued walking.

Then, they bid me enter a rusted-roof house. In that narrow room there was nothing except a piece of stone where someone could sit. One of the soldiers said to the other, "I am going to the other place where the other woman is. You do as you know you should."

He left in a run.

13

Bless those that Curse You

There was nobody but the other soldier and me. My heart started beating loudly in fear.

"Why did they bring me here?" I asked myself. "Why did they leave me here alone with him? Is he going to defile me? Rape me?"

These questions began to trouble me.

"Oh, God! Didn't you promise that we wouldn't be tested beyond our ability?" I began to pray in my heart, "Please God, I don't want this man to defile me. Please, protect me. Please, give me a route of escape."

I wept and prayed in his presence.

The soldier said, "Please, don't weep. I am your brother. My name is Yonas. I am just obeying an order."

"Why did they bring me here?" I asked him.

"I have no clue," he answered me. "I was given an order to punish you till you could bear it no more. But I have sisters like you. Come what may, I will never raise any finger against you. They want to punish you in such a state as you are in! Monsters!" He spoke bitterly.

He continued calmly, "Sister, why do you have to suffer this way? Keep your faith in your heart, and tell them that you have revoked your faith. God sees your heart!"

"It is when you acknowledge God in your heart and through your actions that you show your love and trust in Him," I told the soldier.

The soldier was very bitter, and I could read it in his face. He continued: "You see, I am a member of the Second Round of National Service."

Yonas began to tell me about himself. "I have suffered my whole life. My wife and children have nobody to look after them. I have tried to cross the border into a neighbouring country twice. Once I came back from Egypt, and I was suffering in Wia. For the second time, I was in Assab. I was caught crossing to Yemen. I was jailed for three years. Finally, when they realised that my health was deteriorating, they discharged me from the army for medical reasons."

"I was relieved to be discharged from the army. However, this was short-lived. My family was recovering economically when I was called again. And here I am in this hellish place, suffering."

"Don't lose heart," I started comforting him. It was amazing to be a source of comfort and hope to others while I was still suffering. This couldn't be anything but the grace of God. It couldn't come out of nothing.

At about four o'clock, the other soldier came, accompanied by two others. I saw Yonas, the soldier talking to me, tremble. I realized what shook him so much.

"So, you are laughing and satisfying your desires," the other soldier shouted at him. "We didn't leave you here to flirt but to carry out orders. Out! Useless!"

He came closer to me and struck me on my face.

"Please, my hand is broken!" I screamed so loudly that I felt as if the house would fall on us.

He asked me the usual questions. "Who is funding you? Will you revoke your faith or not?"

They left me in the room as if I were dead.

The next morning, the soldiers found me there, my strength spent. They ordered a car there and returned me to the health facility from which I was taken away.

You see, if God doesn't will it, you won't die. Otherwise, I should have been long dead and couldn't have been alive for the sufferings I endured. I suffered and was about to pass out due to the extreme pain I endured. The cast around my hand was not only dry but very hot in the heat. It began to itch because some infections grew there. I asked them to remove the cast. God is good. A new medical officer assigned there removed it and bound my hand up with a bandage.

A few weeks later, Simon, the brother who came and talked to me in secret, came back again. Each time he visited me, my spirit was refreshed and filled up with encouragement. However, that day he was ashen faced and looked otherworldly. I knew he was bearing some bad news.

"Even now they have beaten you in this state your are in?" He asked. "Why is God still silent? I wish God would ..." He didn't finish his sentence.

"Simon, don't be so bitter" I told him. "Remember the word of the Lord: 'Bless, those who curse you. And pray for those who persecute you.'"

"Yes, you are right about that. But sometimes, ..." He didn't finish his sentence. He began to weep very bitterly. I joined him and began weeping.

"Don't weep," he told me. He started to comfort me. "There will be one day when God will wipe our tears from our faces. Our fleeting sufferings are preparing for us eternal glory."

"Is there anything new?" I asked him.

"One brother has gone to the Lord!" he told me.

"Here?" I asked.

"Yes here," he told me. "He was here in prison for four years. Because of the beatings he suffered, he had poor health. He used to fall ill repeatedly. However, he received no medical attention. Last week, while he was still very ill, they locked him up in isolation and died there."

Simon was weeping.

"He was the father of four," he continued. "His wife left the country when she found life here in Eritrea unbearable. His children are with their grandmother."

I was very sad.

"He is in his Father's arms," I told him. "God will take care of his family."

Simon told me, "You are right. By the way about twenty brothers and sisters have come here."

"From Sawa?" I asked.

"No, from Asmara," he answered. "They caught them in a prayer meeting." He then added, "I met a close friend of mine, and we had a little chat. I am amazed by their faith in the Lord! He also has told me some information."

"What did he tell you?" I asked him.

"He told me about a brother," he said. "The brother was put in prison before the Church was shut down in 2002. He suffered in prison for fourteen years. After they released him, he managed to go to the Sudan, and now he is married. God truly rewards those who suffered for Him."

We thanked God together.

"I must go", he said "I don't want them to catch me here."

And he left.

14

If God were with You

At about dawn, a soldier came and shook me out of sleep. "Hurry up, pack your things," he told me. "You will leave this clinic because you have recovered."

I packed the few clothes I had. He took me by car to a home that looked exactly like the one they had taken me to before. In the house, there were three other young women.

"I have a very terrible pain," I told him. "If it is possible, I want some medicine prescribed for me."

"We don't have medicine for you," he told me. "I wish you were dead!"

He left me there. Half an hour later, he came back and told me, "Let's go."

"Where am I going?" I asked him.

"Shut up! Just come!" He shouted at me. In less than an

hour, he took me to yet another place. I knew that one type of punishment was taking prisoners from one hot place to another hot, desert place.

In my heart, I said: "How about now? Which house will they take me to?"

Angry and calling me bad names, he took me to a prison surrounded by soldiers. The room was very narrow, unclean, and full of dust. Apart from a window and a door, the room had nothing.

The most shocking thing was thinking that a human being must be very cruel and unkind to tell people to stay inside in such hot weather. After my wanderings here and there the whole day, I was completely exhausted. However, because of the extreme heat and the hot weather, I was afraid that I might fall into deep sleep and never wake up. I knew that many people had gone to sleep and had never woken up. But still I fell asleep where I sat down.

I don't know how long I slept. Suddenly, loud laughter and loud voices woke me out of my sleep. "In the Name of Jesus," I said as I woke up. I looked around me but there was nobody there.

Now awaken, I began to pray and sing a hymn. In my prayer, I forgot the place of my suffering and pain and was in a wonderful spirit. As I prayed, suddenly I heard a voice that contradicted the spirit I was in. The voice disturbed me.

"You say, 'God is with me!'" Satan's word flew into my heart like powerful arrows. "If God were with you, why do you experience such suffering?"

He knocked on the door of my conscience repeatedly. I rebuked him, "In the Name of Jesus, go away from me!"

You see, Satan comes as an angel of light. If you are not wary, he is dangerous. Especially in times of suffering and distress, in the time when darkness and death has surrounded you, it is not difficult to understand that he would cause you a lot of suffering and trouble.

"Doesn't the word of God say, 'You will be head, and not tail'? But look at you! You are suffering here. Others who have scored passing grades are studying at college."

Such words were about to plunge me into a spirit of self-pity and grumbling. Such powerful arrows were worse than the actual suffering I was in.

"O God! Help me!" I prayed and began to weep and groan in a low voice. I loudly said, "My God is in Heaven! And He does what He wills!"

I sang and thanked God in that small room. I was amazed as I realized in my spirit Satan left, clothed in shame.

In truth, to praise God in the midst of suffering it is such a divine secret that goes beyond human power. I stayed in that room for five months without the luxury of sunlight. I didn't see anyone except the soldier who brought me food.

Nature poses additional problems for women because of their menstrual cycles. In my time of suffering, this was a big challenge. Due to lack of sanitation, my womb began to give me a lot of pain. However, there was nothing I could do except tell God in prayer. I am amazed when I think how God supported me during the days when I didn't see any human being during those five months of darkness. My hand completely healed. My head was sometimes painful, but that also became better. However, my womb still caused me pain.

One day, I informed the soldier who brought me food about my condition. Thankfully he informed the camp commander about my request, and he sent me some painkillers. Later, however, the chief commander came to know about this, and I was told that he officially ordered that I should receive no medical help.

After these five months of punishment, where I received chastisement in solitary confinement, I was taken to a prison where eleven young women were held. When I saw the women, my heart was greatly comforted, and I thanked God.

One of them was a woman whose name was Tirhas and who came from Sawa to Wia. I went to her and hugged her tightly. I found my beautiful friend, her countenance darkened and her morale gone. She was in very bad misery and had a lot of anxiety. That night, she went to bed without saying a word. I knew the situation was bitter because I was experiencing it myself.

The next morning, Tirhas woke up and told me weeping, "Now it is too long! I don't think God is with us!"

I could see she was angry. It might look to those who are not tested, those who are leading a peaceful and pleasant life, that she had lost her faith in God. However, the heat of Wia could make you lose your faith not only in God but also your faith in His existence. I began to comfort her according to the grace God gave me. After we prayed together, she regained her normal composure. The amazing thing is that once you understand how wonderful the grace of God is, you endure the unusual place as if it were usual, and you live as if you were like other unpersecuted people with normal lives.

15

Meeting My Spiritual Mentor

We resumed the usual task of collecting rocks and gravel. Our bodies had gotten used to the punishment.

One morning, as I was walking to the gravel pit, I saw the face of someone I knew. However, I convinced myself that it could only be a similarity between faces. As I came closer, I was dead sure that I knew that person. As I recognized her, I fell face down unconscious.

It was Hanna, the woman who established me in my Christian walk. Hanna stood there before me. I very much wanted to go and hug her, but it was against the rules. Tears began to flow down my cheeks. I don't know how long I stood on the road. If the soldier had not struck me on my back with his stick, I would have stood there like a statue. I wished the time of our dismissal from work would arrive fast.

"Come what may," I promised myself, "I will go and see her."

In the afternoon, I enquired about the cell where Hanna was staying. Hiding from the guards, I went to her quarter. If God had not protected me and the guards had found out, my punishment could have been severe.

I rushed to her, and I embraced her as a baby would do his mother's breast. The young women separated us forcefully. Hanna's face was flooded with tears. She could not believe the sufferings which I underwent when I told her.

In her turn, she told me that she had lived in Wia for a long time.

Hanna was a member of the *First Round National Service*[9]. For her to be imprisoned for the Lord was a part of her normal life. She often told us to be strong in the Lord and in His mighty power when she taught us about salvation and discipleship.

And now she could see her fruit, one of the students she taught, suffering with her.

I asked her to tell me about herself.

"One day, there was a Christian meeting," she told me. "Suddenly, the police came and took us away. They took us to Adi Abeito, and we suffered there for about six months."

"Some Christians were released when they signed a paper that stated that they had revoked their faith. Others, like me, didn't want to sign it."

"After that, they brought me to Wia. Aster, I don't need to tell you anything because you are suffering likewise."

---

9 The first group of men and women who went to fulfill their national service are called The First Round National Service. They went to Sawa to recieve military training in 1994.

"One day, they beat me until my womb was damaged. On another day, they beat me until their sticks broke on the inside of my feet, and I was more dead than alive. Despite my sufferings, I haven't denied the Jesus I worship. And I will never deny Him. Don't lose heart! If we are alive, we live for the Lord, and if we are dead, we die for Him."

Hanna's face was covered with brown patches. However, her smile went deep into my heart and made it leap with joy as John did while in Elizabeth's womb. Her flesh has weakened. Her spirit and her hope, however, were still strong.

The authorities always ask her, "Who is funding you? Where do you meet? What is the nature of your relationship with Ethiopia and the US? Who are archenemies of Eritrea at the time"

As Jacob's spirit was renewed when he heard the news about Joseph, joy descended on my spirit. Talking to Hanna long into the night, it was nearly four o' clock in the morning. Now, I began to worry how I would get to my place. Hanna, however, knew the path because she had lived in Wia for a long time. She led me to my place and went back to hers. I entered my room without anyone seeing me.

I had only about an hour's sleep. However, I spent it worrying about Hanna. "Have they found her? Or is she safe?" The whistle blew before I went to bed. Before I had a wink of sleep, I got up for a hard day of work.

The sun was so hot that it melted me easily like it does tar. It was a daily occurrence for some young women to fall unconscious, and it was taken as a given. Hanna, like me, went to work without a wink of sleep. I saw her from a distance and winked at her. I very much wanted to meet her again and decided to give her a secret visit as I did the night before.

After we finished our assigned tasks and returned to our places, I waited until darkness fell. After the sun had set and darkness had fallen, my friend and I started on our way to the toilet. After a few steps, we heard a voice, "You stupid women, where are you going?"

Both of us answered him boldly: "We are going to the toilet!"

"Stay there! Cheats! It is enough you are cheating the government and the people, and do you want to cheat us too? Enough of your deception."

He showered us with a lot of bad and obscene names. He whispered to the soldier who stood near him and ordered us, "Follow us!"

My friend and I knew that they wanted to rape and defile us. Praying in our hearts, we told them that we were not going with them. Enraged, both of them punished us severely military style.

After the punishment, they told us to go back the way we had come. To be honest, my heart was filled with bitterness.

"They have punished us very severely," I told my friend. "Should we go back without meeting Hanna? Let's go through the way she showed me yesterday. It is a secret path!"

My friend was disheartened by the punishment, and she refused to go with me. So we returned to our room. I was never as sad as that night.

One week later, my friend and I tried again. Since God facilitated things for us, we met Hanna. In the evening, we went and met her. When she saw us, not only her, but all the young women in the room were shocked.

They knew how dangerous it was to come and visit from another place. Especially, she was very shocked when we informed her what happened to us when we tried to come to her. Out of love, she advised us that we should not try again in the future. She mixed *tihni* and gave it to us to drink. We had a warm spiritual talk for three hours, and she testified to us about things she and other brothers suffered.

Especially when she recounted the things that happened to her, what we bore did not look like sufferings at all to us.

"One day," she told us, "in the Second Offensive [i.e. the war between Ethiopia and Eritrea in 1999] my brigade commander opposed me and other Christian brothers and sisters. And he often told us, 'After defeating the Woyane [the Ethiopian army], it will be your turn.'"

One day, the battle intensified on the wing where Hanna was stationed, and the commander told Hanna and the other Christian brothers and sisters to move forward into the heat of battle.

The male combatants opposed him. However, he wouldn't listen to them. Sensing that it was their fate, the Christian brothers and sisters moved forward, holding their lives in their hands, bombs falling near them and bullets flying by. They went into the midst of a terrible battle, covering for others. The body of one of them could not be found anywhere. Another was wounded and died after a short time. Hanna told us that she was amazed to have escaped with her life from that battle.

In the middle of our chat, I asked her about two people, a young woman and a young man, she had a special relationship with, whom I knew very well. When she told me about them, my tears flowed endlessly.

"One day, his commander found the young man reading a Bible and punished him severely. One day his commanders strapped him in a style nicknamed 'Helicopter.' They tied his hands and feet behind him. Since they strapped his hands for a long time, they were paralyzed. Now, he is handicapped has been discharged from the army and is a businessman."

About the young woman she told us, "Her commander so brought her to the end of her wits through constant punishment that one day she decided to kill him. However, a voice in her heart rang, 'Killers do not inherit the Kingdom of God.' So she repented of her intention, and she gracefully bore her sufferings."

"Another day, a bomb went off in the midst of her unit, and she was injured. Shrapnel hit her and went deep into her breast. She suffered for a long time due to the shrapnel. She was demobilized and started living in Asmara. Then, she had the shrapnel removed in a hospital. However, she didn't feel any better. Some years later, she went to the Lord," she told us.

Hanna gave us much advice about things we should do. She had suffered and had a lot of trouble from the beatings and punishment she received. As she talked to us, I could see her pain was great. Especially when she told us, "I don't think I have much time to live. I think the time has come for me to go to the Lord," my friend and I held her tight.

"We too are going with you," we wept with her. A Christian sister in the room said, "Please, be calm. They might hear us and come," and she told us to stop sobbing.

Hanna adviced, "You will experience a lot of suffering. You will live so that you may tell a story for other generations. But as for me, I don't think I will live long."

She wept as she spoke.

She continued her story, "One day, as we were in a prayer meeting, a sister had a vision about me. In the vision, she saw me wearing a veil like a bride getting married. 'Then, a man in bridegroom's clothing came and took you by hand,' she told me. When she shared the vision, all the sisters there, said, 'In your wedding, I will be bridesmaid. I promise, I will prepare this and that' because they thought I was getting married. But now that I come to think of it, the Bridegroom, Jesus, is taking me home," she told us. All of us said to one another, "God knows what will happen."

Though her story broke our hearts, it certainly made us stand in the faith since it was a source of faith for us. My friend and I returned to our room secretly, our eyes red from weeping.

We prayed to the Lord to strengthen our hearts since we knew that the sufferings our brothers in the faith and we endured was for glory. We prayed a little and went to bed.

Now the authorities came to know that we were visiting Hanna secretly so we had no opportunity to visit her after that. However, we saw each other from afar as usual, and several months passed by.

Eventually, I noticed that three weeks had passed without seeing Hanna, the woman who cultivated me in my spiritual walk. My heart grew heavy. I got worried but didn't know who to ask about her. My friend and I (the woman who shared in my suffering and troubles) decided to do something. We decided to pray so that God would open an opportunity for us to secretly visit her.

We tried three times, and we failed three times. But, God was good. One day, a cultural troupe came to our place to give a show, and we used that occasion to achieve our goal. Acting as if we were going to the show, we disguised ourselves and went to our sister.

We found her in the narrow room, lying on the floor as two women wept holding her hands and her feet. My friend and I called her by her name and came closer to her.

Let alone answer us, she didn't even recognize us. We started praying, and we asked God to heal her according to His will. One of the young women told us that she had told the guards to take her to a medical facility. "But, they refused to listen to us. They just gave us painkillers." The young woman was weeping, "O God! Aren't you alive?"

Hanna was suffering from pain and was in the throes of death. We didn't know what to do. Due to the extreme heat and her high fever, she was suffering and taking her last breaths.

I asked them when she fell ill.

"She has been sick three weeks!" they told me.

One of them said, "They had beaten her in this terrible place three weeks ago. The next day she was unable to walk. One day, the unit commander came and visited her. After a week, we helped her and took her to the clinic. In the clinic, the doctor gave her an infusion, and she became better and was brought back. The next day, she became what she is now. Look at her!"

She wept very loudly.

Hanna, heroine in the faith, gathered her strength and said, "Don't lose heart!"

One of the young women said, "God is good! Look she is talking! Give me *tihni*."

She tried to make her drink the *tihni*. However, the *tihni* flowed down her mouth. Immediately, her body became hard like wood, and she breathed her last.

We screamed very loudly, and the room shook with our voice. Hanna, the good woman, a real Christian, and heroine of the faith, went to be with the Lord, the one she wanted to see, her Lover. I was exhausted due to weeping and sobbing.

My head was splitting with pain. I collapsed where I was.

16

Gone to be with God

Even though I knew that Hanna had gone to the Lord and had no doubt that she was resting in His bosom, her death filled my heart with grief. I didn't eat for almost a week. Due to the injury I sustained, I could not bear my pain. I found it hard to engage in daily activities.

One morning, my legs felt weak, and I was unable to stand up. Except for my friend, Saliem, everyone left and went to their usual activities.

The soldier asked them about Saliem and me. They told him that I was sick.

Angry, he came rushing in and in a threatening tone told us to start moving. Let alone walk, I had no strength even to answer him.

Saliem told him about my condition and explained to him calmly why we didn't go to work. She told him she was unable to leave me alone and entreated him to take me to a medical facility, if possible.

However, he had no concern for us. The only thing he repeatedly said was, "Move on!"

Saliem kept trying to lift me up however, I was unable to stand up, and collapsed everytime she tried.

The soldier then said, "Leave her alone! You come with me!" He threatened her.

"Brother, how can I leave her?" she asked him. "Please, just for today."

She entreated him earnestly, but he didn't listen to her. They left me alone and went out of the room.

In the afternoon, my roommates came back and found me lying in the place they had left me. Thinking I was dead, they shook the room with screams. They took me to the clinic where I was given an infusion.

The next day I became better, thanking God for the help from my jail mates. I stayed in the clinic for three more weeks. After the three weeks, I was told that I had improved and had to return to work. Honestly, if God hadn't showered His grace on me and performed this miracle, it would have been impossible for me to live. I was severely suffering and was very ill.

After we had come back from our usual activity, Saliem said, "There is a letter for you from Asmara."

"A letter? For me? From where?" I pressed her to answer me.

Saliem said, "From your family."

I wept until I almost fainted when she told me it was from my family. Two years had elapsed, and I was entering the third year since I had seen my family..

It was after this long time that I received the letter from my family. Saliem told me I should stop weeping or she would not give me the letter. I became calmer, and she handed me the letter. However, I had no strength to read it, so I asked her to do so for me.

It was Yerusalem, my sister in the flesh and in the Lord, who wrote the letter. The contents of the letter read like this:

"[Peace] from God the Father and our Lord and Saviour Jesus Christ be with you."

"My kind sister, the one I have missed so much and last born of the family. Already, three years have passed. We miss you, your laughter, conversation, and jokes. And now, our family life has become tasteless, like a soup without seasoning."

"I fully understand the kind of suffering and trouble you are in. However, since I know you will not go unrewarded, I am comforted. I am always praying day and night for you that the God of Heaven would give you His grace and power abundantly."

"Nobody in the family had any doubt that you would join college and achieve high status. When everybody started returning but you had not come back, I knew that you must be incarcerated for your faith."

"Our family heard about your imprisonment four months later. It became intolerable for Mother. Father found it hard and didn't know what to do. He left no stone unturned to get you released. He went to different places and met different people. Due to this, his blood pressure rose and his diabetes grew a little worse, and he had to get medical attention in a hospital. Now, thanks to God, he has improved."

"Mother and Father tried to visit you. Once, they were informed that you were in Alaa[10], and Mother and I went there. But, we were told that we had wrong information and could not find you there."

"Finally, Father and our uncle, Colonel Berhane, went to Sawa, where they were informed that you went to Wia, and we came to know about your whereabouts."

"One day, Mother and I started our journey to Wia. But, we were told to return at Massawa. Father approached our uncle, Colonel Berhane, to do something."

"Our uncle was not willing. He told Father that he could do nothing, excusing himself on the pretext that you refused to sign the faith abandonment paper."

"Our family's burden is not just yours. Our brother, your elder and your special friend, was found in a prayer meeting six months ago. He is also in incarceration in Alaa."

"What? What? In incarceration?" I interrupted her reading. Then I told her, "Can you please read that again?"

She read it again for me. "Our brother, your elder, and your special friend, was found in a prayer meeting six months ago. He is also in incarceration in Alaa."

I felt my legs go weak. I also felt as if my head were being severed. We could not finish reading the letter because I had little strength. Saliem put my head on her chest and began to pray for me, rubbing my head.

---

10 Alaa is a prison near Dekemhare where prison cells are in shipping containers.

"Let's go to bed," Saliem told me. "We will continue reading the letter tomorrow."

"No, please finish reading the letter for me," I told her.

She gave in and continued reading the letter.

"I went to Alaa to see him. There are many males and females incarcerated in Alaa. It is amazing. Your elder brother and special friend has a wonderful spirit. When he said 'the sacrifice our family is paying has value' my hear gets comfort and I got he feeling that the Spirit of God must be very powerful on him."

"To be honest, Mother is grieving a lot. However, since she understands that paying a sacrifice for the Lord has value, she is always praying for you so that God would give you grace."

"Our uncles, especially Colonel Berhane, are provoking Father to talk to you to revoke your faith. Our uncle who is living abroad called home three months ago and spoke about a lot of nonsense. He told Father that we were enemies of the country, CIA agents, Woyane operatives, traitors and agitators. He told Father a lot of rubbish until Father was fed up. He said that we were unable to control our hubris and that the Government had given us unparalleled privilege."

"One day, Father got angry, 'Do human beings have no rights? You, though in a foreign land, have your rights respected.' Our uncle gave Father a surprising reply. He told him that there was no country with better human rights than Eritrea and told Father, 'Your daughter deserves it' and hung up the phone. Now, Father has a grudge against him."

"Beloved sister, finally, I would like to leave you with a Word from the Scripture. 'Therefore, since we are surrounded by such a great cloud of witnesses, let us throw off everything that hinders and the sin that so easily entangles, and let us run with perseverance the race marked out for us. Let us fix our eyes on Jesus, the author and perfecter of our faith, who for the joy set before him endured the cross, scorning its shame, and sat down at the right hand of the throne of God.' Consider him who endured such opposition from sinful men, so that you will not grow weary and lose heart."

"Therefore, you and your friends should look at the Lord, and don't let suffering and trouble break you down. Be strong in the Lord and in the might of His strength. You are always in our hearts and in our prayers. Please, tell all the brothers and sisters that are experiencing suffering, 'Be strong!' God be with you!"

After reading the letter, I was unable to sleep. I could not accept the imprisonment of the young man who was not only my brother but also my friend.

In our family, there were six of us children – two males and four females. My eldest brother joined the Eritrean armed struggel before I was born. He was martyred in the Battle of Afabet. Now, I had one brother. For this reason, our family pampered him. I could not imagine how he bore his sufferings.

Father had diabetes, we took special care so that he was not angry for any reason. His doctor had sternly warned him that he had to take care of his health. When my sister told me through her letter that he was sick, to be honest, my gut feelings told me that he was no more.

Our relationship with Father went beyond a child-parent relationship. I also saw the situation Mother was in. Without a wink of sleep, I wept the whole night.

Saliem said, "Aster, aren't you asleep yet? And you are still weeping?"

She came forward and hugged me. "Don't lose heart! You should remember what the word says. 'The troubles of a just person are many; yet God rescues him from all of them.'"

She put both hands on my head and prayed for me. After she prayed, my spirit was revived and felt better. Already it was dawn, and, as usual, we went to our daily punishment.

17

What Superstition is This?

For almost a month, I kept reading the letter from home. My mind was occupied with my family. Is Father still alive? How about Mother? Especially, I was worried about my older brother, who was incarcerated in Alaa, and diligently prayed for him.

When I thought about him, a word of God came to mind: "In this world you will have trouble. But take heart! I have overcome the world." The verse comforted me. I believed that my brother and I would overcome everything because of the power God gave us. In fact, I believed that we would be more than conquerors.

One morning, as usual, we had our breakfast, and I was on my way to the place of punishment when a soldier called me by name and told me to stop walking.

In my heart I said, "What now? What do they want?"

"Let's go! Go!" he told me and followed me as if he were driving sheep. After we walked for some minutes, he bid me enter a place that looked like an office. He told the man sitting at a table, "She is here!"

The man a (I found out later that he was named Colonel Tsehaye) instructed, "Tell her to come in."

The soldier left me with Colonel Tsehaye. Later, I came to discover that the Colonel was the camp commander.

When I went inside his office, I could not believe I was in Wia. It seemed as though we were in Asmara. It had been three years since I last saw a spacious place like this, furnished with an air-conditioner and full of refrigerators. When I saw the commander's office, I realized how selfish and full of injustice some people are. The commander didn't even greet me according to the custom of our people.

He sucked the tobacco in his mouth and said, "If our government were not conscious of people like you – traitors and impotent people – you would have destroyed this country bought with the blood of our heroes. Now you have seen the whip of the Revolution is not short. I hope you have learned your lessons that you can lead a normal life, if you have become a good citizen. Don't you think so?" He moved his feet and shook his head. He was restless.

I didn't even say a word. I just bowed my head and kept quiet.

"Don't you think that the Government of Eritrea became aware about you and your likes just recently? A long time ago, in the Revolution, during the bitter armed struggle, the Front knew about you and your likes and was well prepared for you when independence was achieved. It was only because we were busy in the reconstruction of the nation and in the war, otherwise, you and the Jehovahs should would been uprooted a long time ago."

He glared and glowered at me and continued talking. A Christian song filled my heart: "The Lord is my banner! The Lord is my banner! He flies high on my behalf" I felt some heavenly boldness fill my heart. He continued, "Let me ask you. Prove to me there is God!"

"God is not assessed by the mind and skills of human beings. You and me, His wonderful creatures, are because He is," I told him.

He retorted back, "You call Him, 'God.' And yet, He could not rescue you from our hands! Therefore, the God you worship is useless!"

"The sufferings I receive at your hand," I answered him, "Bring me reward and glory. Therefore, I am glad."

"You mean when you are dead? When your body is taken from here?"

I answered him, "Whether I die or live, it is for God. I have the hope of eternal life, and I receive your punishments and suffer filled with hope."

He contorted his lips.

"What you call suffering and punishments are due to your crimes and your offenses. What do you call eternal life? Nobody has risen from the dead. It is a superstition and a false religion. I am amazed by you! You are young. In addition, you are pretty. Academically, you are one of the top. And you have an excellent character. It is very sad that you should get involved in such unwanted faith – a tool of imperialists such as the USA."

I could see he was very angry. He continued to talk to me in a very serious tone.

"Look!" he said, "It is not because I like you or I want to do you a favour that I have called you here, to my office, and am trying to reason with you. It is because I know your uncle, Colonel Berhane, and because he entreated me to talk to you and convince you. Your father is in a hospital due to your situation. Colonel Berhane wants you to admit your guilt, revoke your faith, and live a peaceful life for your father's sake."

I knew my Father was in a serious condition. When he started talking to me about him, I could not hold my tears. "I won't allow you to weep here. What do you want of us? The choice is in your hand."

He intimidated me to stop my sobbing.

"Now, what is your decision? I will give you a week to think about it and to inform me."

To be honest, I was still young. If I accepted their suggestion, I had the ability to achieve a lot. He had told me that my father was in a hospital as a consequence of my imprisonment. I knew how his spirit would be refreshed if he saw me in the flesh. I also knew that my family was experiencing untold sadness due to my brother's and my imprisonment.

If I were to go back home while they were in such a situation, their hopes would be renewed, and their condition would be normalized. However, it became very difficult for me when I compared these earthly benefits with the rewards and glory of eternal life.

I couldn't abandon for any reason the truth and conviction I found in my inner being through truth and the Spirit. I had decided to make it my glory and my goal to suffer for Christ. The fact that I had taken such a decision at such a tender age couldn't emanate from any other source but from God. That is why I answered him this way, "It is not necessary that I should take a week to think over this matter. I will tell you my decision right now. I will not revoke my faith in Christ. It is this crime that has kept me a prisoner in Wia. If following Christ is my crime, I don't mind receiving punishment until the day of my death."

I could see the expression on his face change. He mocked me.

"What kind of ignorance is this – to pay such sacrifice for what you call Christ, or do you call Him Jesus?" He again said, "Listen, your uncle, Colonel Berhane, will come this week in person. We will see what you will do then! Now, leave! Out! Traitor! Block-head!"

He watched me go out.

The soldier who escorted me to the office took me back. Having finished our work, we returned home. I wept the whole night thinking about my father. I asked my roommates to pray for him.

"O! God! When are you going to end my troubles?" I kept praying.

Three weeks later, a soldier came running to my place. He called me by name, and instructed me to follow him to Colonel Tsehaye's office. I said in my heart, "At least, I will enjoy some cool air." My uncle, Colonel Berhane, was with him sitting in the office. My heart missed a beat. I went and hugged my uncle tightly. The commander left us alone in the office. Tears flooded my eyes. My uncle looked exactly like my father. So I thought I had met my father instead.

"Is my father dead?" I asked him in tears.

"Who said he is dead?" Uncle asked me. "What kind of faith is this of yours and your sister? My brother's home used to be full of peace. Now, you have brought this fruitless faith and have turned it into hell. Your older sister, Yerusalem, due to her faith, suffered a lot in the army! You are repeating her mistake! Fool that he is, your brother, instead of attending his education was found praying in a place which the government has banned! What a cursed people are you?"

He threatened me and tried to intimidate me.

I had argued numerous times with my uncle, Colonel Berhane, about our faith in Christ. He had warned us not to tell him about Christ, and for this reason, he had nearly severed his ties with my family.

Mother is a believer, a follower of Christ. Father believed, "It is right to follow Christ in the faith which one's forefathers handed down to you." He didn't go to church. However, he didn't stop reading the Bible and praying. I had gone to church since childhood. My father never forbade me to do so.

Many told my father to stop us from going to church, but he answered them thus, "Faith is an individual affair while a country is a common possession. I brought up my children in liberty. I will respect their choices."

He had such a wonderful and reasonable stand. For this reason, my father and uncle didn't agree often. Especially, my father was well educated, and he used to grieve about the maladministration in his work. He often argued with my uncle about administration-related issues. Usually they spent hours during the day, and even occasions they spent hours at night for such debates. Problems such as mine undermined my uncle's relationship with our family.

He called me by name and said, "Listen, Aster! I want to know your decision right now! I will take you home in the car I came with. You then can see your father before he dies."

In such a difficult hour, I asked God to help me.

"What can I say about my decision?" I asked him.

"You own your guilt. You inform [the authorities] about the secrets you know. Remember, a country comes before faith and family."

"I have done nothing wrong. My faith is a private matter. I have not stolen anything. I have not wronged anyone."

He interrupted me and said, "What is your decision? I have no time."

I told him, "If you think I will abandon my faith, don't even think of it. You are talking about secrets and crime. I know only one secret. And that is that I am a follower of Christ, and that I am suffering in this desert because I am a Christian."

"Do you know in whose hands you are?" he asked me. He talked angrily, "You don't know that the Revolution doesn't say enough of the blood of people. Don't you know that it has drunk the blood of many? At least, you should know this."

Angry, he stood up. "Is that your decision?"

I said, "That is my decision."

"You are a blockhead! You have no care for your family. You don't know anything about your future. You are dumb!"

He fished out two hundred Nacfa notes and threw them at me.

He called Colonel Tsehaye and said, "Good bye." He left me there. The soldier who escorted me took me back to my place.

18

We have Run Out of Medicine

I didn't get any sleep. I thought the whole night about my father who my uncle said was bedridden. At about dawn, I had a short nap. However, before I had enough sleep, the whistle blew, and I tried to get up. Due to my anxiety and exhaustion, my womb began to hurt, so I was unable to get up. I went back to bed.

A few minutes later, a loud authoritative voice blared in my ears, "You arrogant woman! Is it bedtime now?"

In a faint voice, I said, "Brother, do you have a sister? Can't you understand the problem of women? My womb is very painful. Let me be, just for today," I earnestly begged him.

"Go away" he said. "You live wildly, and finally you harvest the fruits of your wild living and become a burden to us!" He went away, enraged, and loudly cursing. I thanked God. I had a little rest, and I felt better.

In the afternoon, I slowly went to the clinic to ask for some medicine, hoping they would give me some. There was a long queue. So I sat at a raised place in the shade to avoid the sun. From a distance, I saw a Christian sister (who was in prison for a long time) coming toward me.

Here, in Wia, the believers were not allowed to conduct Christian activities, have meetings, or meet with each other. I knew this Christian only by sight. She came closer and gave me a long kiss, as Christians do in Eritrea. God gave us this opportunity, for a chat.

This woman, named Rahel, was sick. So, she was allowed to come to the clinic to get some medicine. Her eyes were puffed up and red with tears. I was not surprised because tears and sobbing were part of the life here in this place. However, I had to ask her, "Are you ok, dear sister?"

She told me, "My sister-in-law is dead."

She continued weeping loudly.

I put my hands on her shoulders and comforted her. "Don't weep!" I remembered my father and said in my heart, "Who knows if my father is alive?" and joined her in her loud weeping.

After we became a little calmer, I asked her, "Was she sick?"

"Yes, she was ill for a long time," she answered me. "It is her son that saddens me most. Poor boy! Now, he is an orphan!"

She wept bitterly.

I asked her, "Is his father, your brother, dead?"

"No," She answered me. "However, he is in prison because of

the Gospel."

I felt saddened, and I didn't say a word.

Rahel said, "My brother is the eldest of the family. He has lived all his life in the church. He was a church minister. My brother was married not a long time ago. The family asked him to get married. However, he didn't listen to the family because he wanted to complete his education and graduate first. He spent almost all his life pursuing his studies. I don't know how he combined both the spiritual and secular education. He received his education abroad in many places. Finally, when he earned his Masters and PhD, he then got married."

"God gave him such a God-fearing woman. You would be surprised to find out how many people wanted his attention. Often, when we sat for lunch, the telephone would start ringing. Our home always had many visitors. I look exactly like him. I received invitations for tea from many people. My kind brother is a God-loving person and loves poeple, and he was a man devoted to his job."

"There is nobody in our neighbourhood who sought help that he didn't provide. When he taught the Word of God, it felt as if the angel of God had come and was talking to you. When he got married and his wife had a child, my parents were overjoyed. To be honest, everyone was happy. However, when the church was closed down officially, we worried a lot, fearing that they would arrest him. My family warned him and often advised him to leave the country. He always gave one answer, "I am ready not only for imprisonment but also to die for Christ."

"Our fears were realized."

"At dawn, we heard the knocking of our door. I rushed to the door and opened it in my nightgown, without a netsela [throw] on my back. I saw a brown car parked outside – just outside our house."

"Three armed soldiers stood near our door, and calling the name of my brother, pushed the door and went inside. His wife and his son were asleep."

"That morning, he was praying and reading the Bible as usual. His wife and my family turned the house into a place of mourning with their screams and weeping. The soldiers took my brother away."

"His son said, 'Daddy, Daddy, I want to go with you!' He wept uncontrollably."

"'Please, let him change his clothes,' we begged the soldiers. But they were not willing to listen to us. They took him away in his night-clothes. To be honest, his imprisonment saddened our neighbourhood. However, nothing could be done."

"After his arrest, his wife's health started to deteriorate much. They didn't even have enough time to express their love for each other. They loved each other greatly."

"They only allowed us to deliver food to him. We were not allowed to see him, though. Some Christians in the prison gave us information. Apart from offering prayers, we could do nothing. Therefore, we always asked God to perform a miracle on his behalf."

"I was imprisoned because a few Christians (I being one of them) were celebrating the New Year in a house. We thought the place was safe, and so we began to pray and sing in a soft voice. At about midnight, as we were preparing to take communion, some police came out of nowhere and surrounded the house. They arrested every one of us."

“I had not received any military training, and therefore, they brought me here. I had no peace, however, about my brother.”

“One day, a trainer in the camp who is from my neighbourhood brought me news from home when he came back from a break. My family sent me word that my sister-in-law was sick. In addition to her illness, it was obvious that she was worried [about her husband] as well. The trainer broke the news to me yesterday.”

I interrupted her story, “Why did he do that? He must be very heartless! Aren’t you going to hear about it sooner or later? Seeing you in such a state, he breaks the news? What cruel people!”

“You are right,” she answered me. “But, I think he did it out of a pure heart. He broke the news to me thinking it might prompt them to give me leave to visit my family in Asmara. He tried to facilitate it for me. His efforts were in vain! It is hard unless God comforted my family with His grace! You know what? Sometimes I don’t understand how God works.”

She finished her story.

In my heart I said, “How many are the sufferings of a righteous person!”

“Go! He is calling you,” she told me. “Please, keep in touch!”

It was my turn to see the doctor. When I told him about my sickness, he told me that they were out of stock, “You have to come back on Monday!”

I prayed in my heart. “Please, I spent the whole day here. At least, give me a tablet so that I may sleep peacefully tonight,” I begged him.

God doesn't let us be tested beyond our capacity.

"Ok, ok, just wait a bit." He gave me a few tablets.

I prayed for the sister in Christ so that she might have a good outcome like mine, and that God would comfort her. I went home, enduring the intense heat of Wia.

On my way home, a powerful word came to my heart:

"But now, this is what the Lord says – he who created you, O Jacob, he who formed you, O Isreal: 'Fear not, for I have redeemed you; I have summoned you by name; you are mine. When you pass through the waters, I will be with you; and when you pass through the rivers, they will not sweep over you. When you walk through the fire, you will not be burned; the flames will not set you ablaze.'"

I felt happiness sweep over my heart. I became glad in my God, and I felt like jumping and leaping. I forgot my pain. In the midst of such suffering and trouble and extreme sadness such incidents were signs that God was with me. The sufferings of my brothers and mine were not humanly possible to bear. However, God helped us, and we were whipped for him, killed, despised, humiliated, saddened, and neglected. Thinking about these things, I arrived at my place in a spirit of relief.

19

A Strange Story of Arrest

I wanted to take the tablet that I had brought from the clinic. However, my roommate was late, and I began to worry about her. After sometime, she came, panting.

"Are you ok?" I asked her repeatedly. "I was worried about you."

She told me she accidentally met brothers and sisters in Christian. While they were sharing her testimony, the time passed quickly that she did not notice how late it is. On her way back, she saw some soldiers from a distance, and she ran to escape their notice. I told her we should go to bed and get some rest. However, she wanted to tell me the testimony the brothers told her. Though I was tired, I wanted to listen so I agreed.

"It is a very surprising story," she began. "One of the brothers told us the story of their Church minister, who is in prison in Asmara."

"One day, group Christians were praying. Some security officers wearing plain clothes came to the place where they were praying and took them to a police station. To release them, the police informed the Christians to provide a guarantor, someone the police could hold responsible in case those Christians were found in a similar situation."

"Some of the Christians asked their parents to be the guarantors for them. Others, however, were afraid of their parents and some could not find their parents immediately, asked the Church minister, to be their guarantor. The Church minister knew how dangerous it was to be the guarantor for another person but as a church minister he was ready to make sacrifices and therefore, went to the police station."

"The policeman asked him, 'Whose father are you?' The minister told him, 'I am the father of all. You see, sir, these are my children. It is for this reason that I have come to be a guarantor for all.'"

"The policeman jeeringly said, 'Who do you think you are that you should be the father of everyone? How many wives do you have to father all these?'"

"The church minister told him, 'I am a minister of the Gospel. Therefore, even though I didn't father them in the flesh, they are my children in the spirit.'"

"The policeman's face turned red in anger, and he hurled innumerable insults and degrading words at the minister. He then called another police officer and told him to lock the minister in a cell. He had gone to be the guarantor for others, but he himself became a victim. For a long time, he was locked in one cell. He was not allowed to leave the cell except during toilet hours. His family always brought him lunch and dinner. Later he was released."

“One day, after his release, he was attending a wedding ceremony of a Christian couple. As a minister, he had to attend and minister in the wedding. Obviously, the people who got the most attention and become the happiest on a day of a wedding are the bride and the groom. In this case, the bride in her wedding dress and the groom in his best clothes added beauty to the place.”

“On that day of their happiness, however, an incident they hadn’t foreseen and couldn’t have imagined occurred. As they were singing and expressing their joy, innumerable police officers surrounded the house. The police turned the wedding house into a house of mourning. The policemen took the bride and the groom, the minister, the minister’s father, and other people to a police station.”

“They took the bride to the police station in her veil?” I interrupted her.

She paused to answer my question. “Yes, they took the wedding couple and others. They took everyone together. Then, they took some people, including the minister, to Sawa.”

“In Sawa, they took them in a prison called Enda Shadushai (the Sixth). We knew how bad the prison in Sawa was from firsthand experience. Therefore, it was not necessary that we should talk about it in detail.”

“I was heartbroken for the couple who were taken to prison on their greatest day. Then, the church minister was imprisoned for more than one year before he was released.”

After a while though, some security people came to his house and took him away again. Until now, he is still in prison.”

“One day I heard some people who were imprisoned with the

ministry described his as a 'hero, someone who doesn't flinch from his faith, a person of strong faith, a man who is a source of comfort for us during our time of suffering.' When we heard this testimony we understood that despite our suffering we had to be a source of hope and comfort for many."

"Other brother shared another testimony. One day when he was carrying food to a prisoner, an elderly woman came to the police station carrying food for her son because he was also incarcerated in that prison. The woman was the mother of two martyrs. She had not seen this son for many years. That day, her waist girded with a *netsela* [throw], she asked the commander of the station to allow her to see her son before she died. The sad thing was that the commander didn't care about the woman. 'Woman, I said leave!' he humiliated the woman. She begged him saying 'Please, for the sake of my martyred son!' However, there was nobody that would listen to her. She didn't see her son, and she passed away still missing him."

"Her son is one of the known Church ministers. He had spent many years in prison, and his health was deteriorating. He asked the authorities to allow him to see a doctor. However, they didn't allow him."

"One day, they took him to a health facility. The doctor who saw him was very surprised. He didn't understand how the patient could still be living. The doctor informed the authorities concerned about the patient, but they didn't care. The brother began to get worse, and his health began to deteriorate fast. His pain became unbearable, and so they took him to see a doctor again. Their intention was, however, to kill him using surgery as a pretext."

"As luck would have it, there was an expatriate doctor who told the authorities that the patient should not be operated on. He told them he would certainly die if he got no essential care. The members of the security gave the doctor's warning a deaf ear. They took him in a covered car to his relative's house and dumped him there. They were hoping that he would die soon."

I asked what happened to the minister. She said the brother who was sharing the story himself was arrested and did not know what happened after that. As she told me this story, I thought that crimes against Christians have not been reported. However, it doesn't mean that they have not been perpetrated.

She continued.

"One of the Christians among the group was a woman and this is what she shared. She had an uncle, whom she loved very much, incarcerated in prison. Her uncle, Solomon, graduated from the University of Asmara with high distinction, and the university employed him as an assistant lecturer. He taught at the university for only four hundred Nacfa [about 20 USD] a month. Luckily, he got a scholarship, and so he went abroad."

"Abroad, he successfully completed his education and came back with a master's degree. Then, he continued teaching at the university. You see, Solomon could have worked in the country where he got his master's for a much better salary. However, he taught at the University of Asmara for only four hundred Nacfa per month."

"After some years, he got another chance to further his education. Therefore, he went abroad a second time. A few years later, he completed his studies for his doctorate degree and came to Eritrea to conduct his research."

"Some time ago, some Christians were caught praying in a house. These Christians confessed to the police that one of the leaders was Solomon. The security forces interrupted his research and used this information as a pretext to arrest him."

"A government official interceded on Solomon's behalf and informed the security officials about Solomon's research and that he was sent abroad for further education by the government. Finally, he secured Solomon's release."

"You see he was about to finish the rest of his research. He was planning to leave abroad to defend his dissertation, and so he was preparing for his departure."

"Suddenly, he was called to a police station. Without a trial, they sent him away to many years imprisonment. The purpose was to target him, to destroy his morale, and to frustrate his dreams, thus distracting him from his ambition."

"The sad thing was his education, which he was dreaming to further, would have helped and benefitted the country and the people who were mistreating him. Solomon could have worked in the countries he had studied. He had a number of good opportunities to secure employment that would have paid him thousands of dollars a year, and they would have treated him wonderfully. Instead, he returned to Eritrea intending to serve his country and society. Ironically, however, he suffered for many years in prison in his own country."

She concluded her story. I felt very saddened by the story I heard. We bore a lot of suffering and trouble for Christ, and I realized that the grace we received was great.

Before bed, we held each other's hands and prayed for the Christians in prison and in distress. We laid down to sleep in our place. It was so hot that it felt as if a volcano had erupted there, and it smelled of fire.

20

A Heart Breaking Story

After a few months, three sisters and I were called before a group of four soldiers. One of them was the man we knew from previous intimidations.

"Today, you are here so that you may tell us your final decisions and give us all the information you know."

His tone was intimidating and full of rage.

We gave him no answer but kept quiet. A soldier looked me in the eye and said, "Why did you choose a faith that your parents didn't know?"

I knew he wanted to scare me.

I retorted, "I don't understand your question. What do you mean?"

"What benefit is there in the new faith of the *pente*?" he asked me. Even then, his rage had not subsided.

I had heard this question innumerable times. So, I didn't care much to answer him and remained silent. They wasted about four hours asking us useless questions.

One of us, strong in the faith and a minister of the Word, boldly told them, "We believe in the Christ who gives life. We have done nothing wrong, and we have not committed any crime."

One of them struck her on the back with the butt of his gun, and she fell down. He said, "In Eritrea, there are only two legal religions. You are guilty of breaking this law, disturbing the peace of the country, and cooperating with the enemy to divide it through the tool of religion. You all deserve to die."

He was very angry.

We still gave him no answer.

After that, one of them said, "Now, we want your final decisions. Who are these people who fund you? And who supports you with the preparation of your teaching and with the organization? What is the name of the manager of the organization that funds you from the US?"

He bombarded us with a lot of nonsensical questions.

I got a little bit angry and said, "This is my fourth year in this camp. You have asked us these questions a thousand times. We have given you our answers. But if you want to hear it again, we are followers of Christ. We know no secret except God. We have no hidden agenda."

What followed was very painful and hard to endure or even describe. The four of them beat us until we were wet with our blood. After a few hours, they dragged us like dogs and left us in an underground room.

The whole day and night we shook the room with our painful cries. A Christian sister fainted in our midst. She didn't hear nor feel what was going on around her. Uncared for, she died there. She was released from pain and imprisonment and now is resting in her Father's bosom.

In such dire circumstances, we had no strength to weep. In fact, due to the extreme pain we experienced, we had great desire to go where she went. After a few hours, some people came and took her body away. This dear sister temporarily was separated from us. We are sure that we will live together in our Father's house.

My friend and I lived in imprisonment in that underground room for many months. One day, I was near death due to the intense pain I suffered. I was allowed to get medical attention in that place where there was little help.

Here, God allowed me to meet someone who suffered in ways similar to mine. Nahom was serving his punishment as a medic for he had a medical education. He did everything possible to help me secretly or openly when he treated me. He was in his thirties and sacrificed his life for the sake of Christ and received all kinds of sufferings innumerable times.

When he related to me his sufferings, I realized how great God's grace was on him.

One day, he told me, he was returning home from work. Two people in civilian clothes dragged him out and put him in a car. They took him to a beautiful villa. There, they shackled him to the leg of a bed for five months.

His parents got worried and didn't know whom to approach for information. The undercover men asked him how many people he smuggled out of Eritrea to the Sudan. They compelled him to show them the e-mails he sent and other things. Their tortures became even worse when they found out facts that were Christian in nature. Finally, they let him go without a word of apology. They strongly warned him that he should say not even a word to anyone about what happened to him.

He wept as he told me about an incident more unbearable than his sufferings. Nahom had a fiancée whom he loved very much. Their love for each other and their harmonious relationship earned admiration from the brethren. They wanted to get married when they came to know each other. However, since he was about to complete his education, they decided to postpone their wedding for a little bit longer.

After graduation, the wedding had to be delayed because the young woman's family had some objections. They knew he was a born-again Christian. So, convincing them took some more time. Later, when things settled, the two families agreed that the two get married.

As they were getting prepared for their wedding, he was the best man in another Christian's wedding. When the festivity of the wedding was in progression, the people began to sing a Christian song. Some people who were watching them, however, went and informed the police. The police arrived and took some guests from the wedding, as well as the bride and the bridegroom, to the Fifth Police Station.

The families of the couple begged the police. They later let the bride and the groom and some close relatives of the couple go home on bail. Nahom and other Christians, however, were not released.

After sometime, the police locked Nahom and others up in the prison in Mai Temenai for six months. After that, they transferred him to Wia where I met him. The sad thing was things were ready on both the bride's and the groom's side to hold the wedding which was only a week away. Though the families of the couple complained about the situation, nobody heard their complaint. The wedding was finally cancelled.

As time passed, the family of the young woman began to pester her. She was unable to bear the pressure of her family and the separation of her fiancé so she crossed the border and (after a terrible time) arrived in England. With the help of a relative, she sent him two or three letters and some money. Her parents kept their pressure up and insisted that she get married, even when she was distant from them.

Finally, Nahom came to know that she had married and bore a child. This broke his heart. Since he loved her much, it was difficult to bear. He felt betrayed, and this controlled his heart. I told him that to suffer for Christ included not only suffering here, in Wia, but also separation from people whom we liked and loved. Especially, I told him the word of the Lord, "Anyone who loves another more than me is not worthy of me." I also comforted him by saying that he should see his fiancée's decision from a realistic point of view.

To be honest, it is very hard to lose someone you loved and considered for a spouse. However, as long as it is for Christ, the reward in Heaven is so great.

In those days when I was in the clinic, I consoled and supported him, and he solaced and supported me in turn.

Yes, they pressed us here beyond measure, but we were not crushed. Sometimes, due to extreme beatings, suffering, pain, and longing, we were perplexed. But, we didn't lose hope. We were persecuted; they mistreated us, jeered at us, and we were pushed to death, but we were not destroyed. As the Apostle Paul said, "We always carry around in our body the death of

Jesus, so that the life of Jesus may also be revealed in our body. For we who are alive are always being given over to death for Jesus' sake, so that life may be revealed in our mortal body."

Through the years, though my friends and I had spent bitter lives; due to God's grace, our spirit had not given in. Though we saw our beloved sisters being taken from our midst by death, we didn't entertain, even for a second, the idea of whether to deny the Saviour or not. We had no clue when we would be released from this hell, but we understood this: whether in life or death, as always we would be with Christ.

One mid-morning, a soldier came and angrily ordered me to pack whatever I had.

In my heart I said, "What do I have to pack? I don't have much, do I? What now? What do they want of me?" I thought about these things for a while.

After some hours, he came back and asked, "Have you finished packing?"

Honestly, I felt irritated.

"What things do I have to pack?" I told him. "I have nothing to pack."

"Let's go!" he shouted at me. "Shut up and let's go! Stubborn woman!"

21

Injustice in Dekemhare

I kept thinking about, "What now? This time where are they taking me?"

He then took me to the office where I was always taken for investigation and interrogation. The interrogator arrogantly asked me, "Do you know why we have called you?"

I had no answer for his question. Therefore, I kept quiet and didn't say a word.

"Very good!" he said. "It has been four years since you came here. Now, you have served your time, and we are sending you home to Asmara. However, this depends on your choice."

I had no doubt that their words were full of deceit and disinformation. For this reason, I waited attentively for the words he would say next with a bowed head.

Then he said, "Now, for the last time, before you go to your family, you will sign this paper that you will not have anything to do with this faith, that you will return to the religion of your fathers you abandoned, and you will abide by the rules and regulations of the government."

He handed me a pen and the paper to sign.

I believe that the sufferings I have endured (the sufferings I have voluntarily endured out of my free choice, following Christ, and accepting the consequences of my choice) have rewards. Therefore, I was not surprised by the words he stated which I had heard innumerable times like unwanted music one is forced to listen to.

I quietly returned the paper to him. Due to the beatings and physical pain, I was unable to say even a word. Therefore, I shook my head and scowling, I showed with my hands my unwillingness to sign the paper.

In a soft voice I said, "I am not going to sign this. I didn't sign it in the past. I am not going to do it today. If you come and ask me tomorrow, my answer is one and the same. I will not sign it."

He rose from his seat and slapped me on the face. In a rage he ordered, "Take her away!" They took me and my belongings to an underground room, where two other young women were locked in a place commonly called 'Under.'

I was not surprised by this because I had lived before in similar places for four years. However, this was different from the previous once. Our bodies had acclimatized to the heat of Wia, the heat that seemed to rise from the ground.

This room was much worse and more confined than the other rooms. However, even in such a place, God had not taken away his grace from me. The two young women I found there were incarcerated for their faith. Though I had heard that they were in Wia, I had never came across them in person. But now, the time had come, and because God willed it, I met them. Together we prayed and comforted each other.

The most amazing thing was, though we were in suffering and distress, we prayed for others who were suffering and imprisoned for the sake of God.

After sometime talking, I told them that my brother was also in prison in Alaa.

One of the young women, Samrawit, who came from Alaa, told us about the suffering our brothers were enduring there. I listened to her attentively because I very much wanted to get information about my brother. She also told us about some Christian women that were incarcerated in Alaa.

Samrawit told us about some *Fourth Round National Service* graduates who were serving in the Construction Department in Dekemhare [a town 45km south of the capital Asmara]. The officials strictly followed these women because they were Christians. As part of their routine, the young women fellowshiped together, drinking coffee, praying and studying the Word of God.

One day, some young men joined them. Some people were spying on them and their activities and informed the police. The police took them away to a court. In sham court proceedings, the judge pronounced them guilty for their Christian activities. The puppet judge had no choice, and so he delivered them over for punishment.

The prison officials wanted the young women for themselves as sex partners. Each claimed one as his partner. They openly talked and boasted about this.

The officials imprisoned the three young women in a one-room mud-brick house. They were not allowed to leave the room at all. The Christian women were not even allowed to bow their heads in prayer or read. Therefore, they did all their Christian activities secretly under the bed sheets. They brought the women food, which was water-soaked lentils, twice a day. The young Christian women had a hard time eating the food.

Then, the officials called them from their room and asked them lots of nonsensical questions. They told them to deny their faith. However, the women rejected the request, and so they handcuffed them with their hands behind them. They beat them with sticks and forced them to stay in the sun the whole day.

Sometimes when the women went to use the toilet, some Christian men would give them food and milk secretly.

One day, a soldier caught them receiving food and milk from a Christian man. In shock, they didn't even try to hide the food and milk.

The soldier ordered them, "What are you doing here? Hurry up, go to your toilet and come back quick!"

The soldier left immediately. As God blinded the Syrians, he darkened the soldier's eyes, and so he did not see what was in their hands. God had delivered them.

One day, a woman, who was labelled an absconder, was added into their number. One of the prisoners often witnessed about the Gospel to her. However, the woman always argued back with the Christian woman and mocked her for her faith.

On one occassion, the Christian woman and the absconder

were discussing the Word of God outside their room. The Christian told the other woman that God could only be found by faith, not by sight.

As they argued, they saw a bright light approaching them. They thought it was the soldiers, and they said, "Woe to us!" They were terrified. The light became brighter and brighter, but there was no human being behind the light. Then, the woman, amazed by what she saw, declared, "I saw Jesus. This is a sign from heaven that God has given me," and she began to weep. This way, the woman met the Lord Jesus Christ and made Him the King of her life. God was working through his children even in dark places by performing miracles and, at the same time, building the faith of the Christians under suffering.

One day, one of the Christians fell very ill as she had lost a lot of weight. She was admitted to a hospital. At this time, her family came to know that she was incarcerated and ill and that she was in a hospital due to her illness. They came to visit her, carrying necessities for her.

Her family talked to the commander. He tried to convince them that their daughter was a traitor and a criminal who followed an illegal religion. He especially told her father that his daugher was found reading the Bible. They had taken the Bible from her and burned it. They threw the ashes away. Her father was shocked.

Later, he entreated his daughter to obey her commanders. He reasoned with her saying, "Listen, these people are not afraid to burn the Bible. I have no doubt that they will kill you."

The most disturbing thing was that they took away what her family brought her.

Samrawit continued, "The legs and hands of these Christian

women had been beaten repeatedly. The consequences of their incarceration was visible in their health. After one year of incarceration, however, they were released only because God said it was enough."

Samrawit concluded that "These times are of being built up in the faith and of the knowledge of God. In these days of suffering, we are close to God and His Word."

When I heard the story, I asked her if she had any information about the male prisoners. When I found out that she knew about their situation, I asked her to tell me their condition.

However, we were very tired, and she promised to tell me more the next day. Certainly, it was God's sustaining grace that one remained faithful to God in such bitter and testing times of suffering.

22

More Suffering

The soaring temperature of Wia almost melted us, as heat does tar. It was more unbearable than the physical and psychological punishment we endured. Since the room I was incarcerated in was an underground cellar, the high temperature made the atmosphere of the dungeon more uninhabitable. My body became covered with a rash.

In my entire life, I never had liver spots or solar lentigines. Now my face was covered with such burnt, discolored skin patches. But, above all, due to the lack of hygiene care, I suffered from a severe itch. Except for our toilet time, we spent our days and nights locked in the secluded dungeon. However, though we were surrounded by a cloud of suffering and distress, by the grace of God, we didn't stop praising Him and praying. Grumbling, hopelessness, and despair had no place in us.

I asked Samrawit about the prison of Alaa and to tell me about the male prisoners and their sufferings. She told me Alaa had innumerable prisoners, including absconders and others. She told me, "There were many young men and women who were caught praying in Mendefera [a town about 60 km south of the capital Asmara] and brought there. In Alaa, there was a man known as Wedi Ghile who beat up prisoners and encouraged his soldiers to do the same."

"Due to his extreme cruelty, people shook and trembled in terror when they saw him. There was a place called Mesqel (the Cross). Believers especially were tortured in a unique way at this spot. Here the soldiers tied both hands of the believers to a wooden beam and let them suspend loosely, leaving their lower part dangling free and their feet barely touching the ground. This way they tormented them so severely till they shed tears of blood."

I thought how my brother would bear such a horrible suffering.

Samrawit continued, "They tortured the men till they could bear it no longer. It was obvious some had gone to the Lord as a result of the intensity of the suffering."

"One day," Samrawit continued her story, "The soldiers tied a brother's hands behind his back. Though he cried and groaned from excruciating pain, nobody gave him any attention because Wedi Ghile's instructions were strict."

"A soldier saw the brother's suffering and went to Wedi Ghile and earnestly entreated him. So, Wedi Ghile ordered his soldiers to untie the brother's hands. The brother's arms, however, were broken, and he had fainted."

"After that, they took him to the hospital. He was informed that unless he underwent a surgery that could only be done abroad due to the level of damage to his arms, one of his hands would be paralyzed."

Then, we prayed fervently in the presence of God for the believers in Alaa.

One of the two sisters, Selam, who shared the same underground room with me and Samrawit, was in prison for the second time due to her faith.

While she was in the National Service, she was put in prison in her duty area for her faith. She suffered more, however, not from physical punishment but from other means of torture. For instance, she was ordered to go on night watch, a woman among men. She could not bear the memory of those terrible days.

Her commanders intentionally ordered her to go on night watch with an officer of some rank. Many times he tried to rape her.

One night as they were on duty, he grabbed her and forcefully tried to rape her. She shook the place with a scream. Scared and ashamed, the officer stopped before going too far. God saved her from his hands.

She was tested in this way, and her soul suffered intensely.

If one met believers in Wia, the testimonies and the stories people tell would be hard to believe. Sometimes it seems such stories are only possible in movies and plays because it is too hard to believe this could happen to real people.

I spent five years in Wia. In those five years, the mercy and faithfulness of God was much more abundant than the sufferings I had borne. I had no doubt the reason I survived such a hellish place was to tell of the glory of God and the story of my martyred brothers.

I didn't know how long I would stay in this terrible place, but I knew one thing: though mountains move and hills were removed from their places, the mercy and peace of God would not be removed from me. Though I saw no clouds and I didn't observe the winds blow, I had no doubt that my God was faithful and would have me freed from this place at the appointed time. My slogan and the slogan of my brothers was one and the same: "If we live it is for the Lord, and if we die it is for Him."

One day, I began to vomit all the food I ate. You see, we ate the food they gave us because we had to. Not only was it tasteless, but it was also undercooked and unhealthy. As a result, our stomachs were always under stress and developed ulcers. I lost weight considerably. Without exaggeration, I went out for toilet only once a week.

This condition lingered for about a month and two weeks. Samrawit and Selam propped me up, fed me, and made me drink water to keep me hydrated. Both of them lost hope and waited for the day when I would be called home to the Lord. My condition deteriorated. I was unable to talk, and I collapsed.

After sometime, I was taken to the clinic. I don't know how many weeks I spent there. The only thing I knew and repeatedly heard was the phrase: "Why don't you kill her?" However, I heard a mightier voice in my heart: "You won't die. You will declare the glory of God."

A fairskin, thin young man's voice rang in my ears: "Don't be discouraged! God has helped you, and the worst is over!"

I didn't pay much attention to his words because I was still weak. When he said it again, and especially when I heard the word "God," I thought it was the voice of an angel and not the voice of a human being.

Once again, he said, "Don't be discouraged! Don't be afraid. I am your brother in Christ."

After some days, I found out that the brother who was giving me treatment was the friend of the young man who visited me in the clinic sometime back. We had an opportunity to talk, and I asked him about his friend.

He kept silent for some moments and then said, "He is fine. But he is a bit busy." But I felt something was wrong. I pressed him to tell me the news. He said, "Sometime ago, he and some other Christians were trying to escape. Some were killed by the bullets fired at them, and some were caught. I have confirmed that he is not among those caught. Therefore, he must be one of those killed." He broke the news to me then and there.

I had no strength to weep and sob, but I felt my heart break as if it were glass shattering on the ground. I said, "Why didn't he have a little more patience?"

He said, "I am surprised by your patience and the patience of your friends. How can one have patience in this place?"

He continued, "By the way, is there God?" He then asked me, "Do we sin more than other people that we have to bear such sufferings?"

It was normal to ask such questions there, where we were. He added, "Aren't the number of people incarcerated in underground dungeons and prisons innumerable? Woe are we!"

He took a deep breath.

In a weak voice I said, "There is a time for everything! God in

His own time will put an end to these things!"

He answered, "I want to leave before the beasts come. I wish they would send you to another place where you can get better treatment. I can see your health is not in its best form. Why don't you do what they want, sign the paper, and pave the way for you to get better medical attention?" He gave me his brotherly advice.

I answered him, "My soul has borne a lot of suffering. I see no reason why I should look back. Whether I live or die, I promise again before you and in the presence of God not to listen to their plea."

"May God help you!" he told me and left the little room, It was called a clinic, but it was very sparse.

I experienced intense pain the whole night. My strength failed me completely. I was going in and out of consciousness. This one was unlike anything I had experienced before. My soul threatened to leave my body. I could find no strength even to cry for help. I felt myself fall off of my bed and hit the ground. Then, I lost consciousness completely.

23

My Father's Death

For two days I didn't regain consciousness. On the third day, I began to feel things a little. Though I didn't know if this was a dream or real, I observed a man dressed in white and his face bright as light standing before me and smiling at me. He came closer and began to touch my head.

Against this man stood someone in ragged clothes who stared at me and screamed at the top of his voice, "You will die! And I will eat your flesh and drink your blood."

The man dressed in white, undisturbed by the threats of the other man, sat beside me and smiled at me. The man who threatened me, enraged and screaming at the top of his voice, left quickly.

The one in white encouraged me, "Don't lose heart! I am with you till the end of the world! The one who remains faithful to death, he will wear an everlasting crown, in the house which I have prepared. Therefore, stay steadfast! Stand in the faith!"

He disappeared immediately.

I regained consciousness immediately after that. In a feeble voice, I said, "Water! Water! Please, give me water."

I didn't know who the person was but I felt someone prop me up, support me, and give me water. After that, I fell into a deep sleep.

The next morning, a staff member of the clinic gave me an infusion bottle. Slowly, my strength began to return. However, I was unable to get down off my bed.

Three weeks later, I began to walk with the support of other people, and sometimes I went to the toilet on my own. Nevertheless, my condition was deteriorating. The people who tortured me, Samrawit, and Selam expected me to pass away.

As I was in such a trying situation, the commander of the camp, Colonel Tsehaye, allowed me to go to Massawa [a port city about 115 km north east of the capital, Asmara] for treatment. I realized that this didn't happen out of the goodness of his heart or because he cared about me but because God sent this miracle to me like manna from heaven. After five years, I began to prepare to leave for proper medical treatment.

I was admitted into a hospital in Massawa. Though I didn't get excellent medical treatment, it was a hundred times better than the nominal treatment I received in Wia.

At the hospital, a nurse, Sister Freweini, began to regularly visit and care for me. I realized from the feelings on her face that she very much wanted to know about my situation.

One day, she secretly gave me a leaflet. The leaflet had only five pages and was entitled "Embaba Tsigereda ab Maekel Eshok" ('The Rose Among Thorns'). The leaflet spoke about the beautiful rose that was surrounded by thorns. Especially, a sentence stayed in my mind: "Some grumble because the rose flower has thorns; others, thank God because among the thorns grow some flowers."

I thanked God for the flowers that grew out of the thorny situation I found myself in. The sister bravely told me about life after death. I heard her through.

After she finished, however, I asked her a question. "Sister," I addressed her, "How do you know I won't inform the authorities that you are preaching to me, disregarding your care for sick people?"

Sister Freweini smiled and said to me, "I know I will have to pay a price for preaching the Gospel. I have no reason to fear those who can only kill the flesh but I fear the One who can throw people out and kill people in hell. Therefore, I am ready. Only may you be ready to accept the Truth and decide to live with Him."

I told her to hug me and give me a kiss. She gave me a kiss and wept. I told her my story. Tears flooded her face.

After she came to know about my condition, she promised me that she would find out about my family. She also promised to pray for me.

After the diagnosis, I was told that I had developed a severe stomach ulcer, that my liver was affected, my womb had developed an ulcer, and that my weight had fallen far less than normal. I had a hard time taking the tablets prescribed for me. Especially, due to the fact that I did not eat much food, the nurses had a hard time inserting the infusion tube. They found it hard to find my veins.

Sister Freweini told me that the other nurses and the two or three doctors used to wonder and felt saddened by the torture I endured.

According to her promise, Sister Freweini told me that she had got news for me about my family and that they would come to see me. I could not control my joy. On the other hand, I was worried about the bad news I might hear of my father. I couldn't take out of my mind my warm-hearted family, the family I grew up surrounded by. When I would really miss my family, I exhorted myself to look toward my Heavenly home so that I didn't wallow in self-pity.

"What are my father, my mother, and sister going to say when they see me?" This thought gripped my mind.

One afternoon, Sister Freweini came with two other people to the room where I was sleeping. I was shocked and lay still like a log. Words failed me. My tears dried up like a dry well. My mother and my sister hugged me tightly. The room turned to a mourning house for about one hour. The nurse rebuked my mother and my sister. All words failed me, I could not speak and was like a dumb person. My mother's beauty was erased, and she had lost her allure. My sister was full of liver spots on her face. I was afraid to ask about my father. They said nothing about him.

So that we might eat from the food they brought, mother made a sign to my sister to open the bag. I stretched my hand to eat food my mother prepared. At this time, I remembered Hanna's words, the words of my mentor and teacher in the faith, who passed away in martyrdom in Wia. She used to say, "I miss my mother's enjera (bread), especially the shiro [stew made of peas and different spices] she made!"

Hanna, the heroic sister, passed away wishing only that she

could eat food her mother prepared and went to the place where heavenly manna is served. For my part, I was eating food my mother prepared because of the grace of God. As I ate, tears began to flow down my cheeks. Mother said, "Don't cry, dear child", but she didn't stop weeping herself.

After the meal, my first question was, "Why didn't my father come?"

My sister answered, "He didn't get permission from work. He begged them, but they refused."

I knew her words were not true.

I began to weep, "Father!" Yet again, we turned the room into a house of mourning. Sister Freweini, the nurse, was angry with us. I knew that my father was dead. I implored them to tell me. I told them that I had seen a lot of suffering and death. I asked them in the name of God not to lie to me. Tears flowing down her cheeks, Mother said, "Your dad has gone to the country he has missed and to the God he had acknowledged as God and Lord on bended knees."

To be honest, I was filled with lots of questions. "Why? Why Lord?" I was inconsolable. Sister Freweini put her hand on my head and began to pray for me. She quoted a verse for me: "I know that you can do all things; no plan of yours can be thwarted."

I became a little calmer, but news of the death of the father I loved, my friend and my dad, sank into my bones. I spent the night in tears and mourning.

The next morning, they told me that my father had had poor health since the day he heard about my imprisonment and especially since the imprisonment of my brother. But I was very comforted when I heard that Father was proud of me for the decision I had taken. Just as for Hagar in the desert, as she was about to die due to lack of water and because she was bitter and didn't want to see her son die before her eyes, God struck a rock and gave her water and a great deliverance and consolation, so when I heard such news in a desert, I felt that a well of consolation was opened for me.

Mother, unable to bear my situation, and as a mother, said, "Do you think they will let you go when you are discharged from the hospital?"

I responded in the manner of Ezekiel's answer to God. As God asked Ezekiel, "Can these bones live?" and Ezekiel answered God, "You alone know!" so I answered my mother, "God only knows." For her question was beyond me to answer.

I asked them for news of my brother. "He is experiencing the same kind of sufferings as you do!" my sister explained without going into specifics.

They stayed with me for three days. All this happened because of the cooperation of Sister Freweini, the kind nurse.

After three days, some people came to know about what was happening. It was dangerous, and my mother and my sister were told to leave. After years of separation, they left before I had had enough of their company.

As they left, my sister said, "This letter is from our father, which he wrote before he died. You read it." She hugged me tightly and sobbed loudly. My mother had sadness beyond measure as she kissed me goodbye.

I opened the letter my father had written.

24

My Father's Letter

To be honest, when my mother and sister left, I felt lonelier than I had ever experienced before in my life. This spirit controlled my heart and mind to such an extent that I was unable to pray. I clung on to the letter from my father as if I were a child who had received a gift. I felt the letter was the image of the father I loved so much so I could not take my eyes off it. My tears flowed down my cheeks. I could muster no strength to open the letter. So many times, I decided to open it, but my hands became cold as if they were steeped in ice. Sometimes I stretched my hands to open it, but I shook all over. So I told mysef to be calmer and tried to sleep. However, no sleep would come. The letter remained unopened for three days.

Sister Freweini hadn't come back since my family left. I was worried over her absence and very much wanted to know what had happened to her. I didn't know who to ask. A number of questions crowded my mind. Is she on leave? Or have they arrested her because they came to know of our relationship and the kindness she has shown me?

While I was in such a state of mind, two undercover security agents and a soldier came to my room. They greeted me with stern faces and told me that they were from the security services.

One of them asked, "Who has given you a visit?"

It was a familiar arrogant posture.

I knew things were going wrong. Therefore, I bravely answered him, "A doctor and some nurses."

The man in military clothes said, "Use your city tricks with others! Who gave you a visit from Asmara? Answer just this question! Don't try to derail us from our purposes!"

I bowed my head. I gave him no answer. The soldier in an angry tone roared at me, "I am talking to you! Answer me! Who was here? I don't think you forget that your very life is in our hands!"

Even then I gave him no answer. One of the three said, "Is it true? Weren't your mother and sister here?"

I told them the truth. "Yes, they were here."

The soldier asked me, "Who informed them that you are here?"

I told him, "I don't know. I have no idea."

The man in military clothes threatened me, "Listen! We don't want to talk much! We would like to know whom you have contacted since your admission to the hospital and what information you have given your family. We want all the details. Otherwise, we will shed your blood as if it were a sheep's before you leave the hospital."

I bravely answered him, "I know that my family came to visit me after five years of suffering and distress. I know this is a miracle from God. I forgot my pain and suffering because of my family's visit. However, to the extent that I am joyful I am grieving my father's death. I know nothing and don't want to talk beyond this. You can intimidate me all you want, but I know nothing else."

One of them mentioned Sister Freweini and said, "You are very arrogant! How is the nurse related to you?"

I knew then that I had endangered Sister Freweini.

The soldier menaced me, "If you mention that your family was here or if your family says anything about you in Asmara, you will experience our long hand all the more." And they left.

I didn't stop thinking about Sister Freweini who had helped me with many things. She had told me that she was the mother of three, that her youngest was only two years old, and that her husband was in Adi Keih [a town 60 miles south east of the capital, Asmara] in the National Service.

The Secret Service had established that Sister Freweini got to know me and that she had contacted my family for me. I had no doubt that the measure they would take against her would be very harsh, but I didn't stop praying that God would help her.

In Sister Freweini's place, another nurse began coming and giving me injections. I wanted to ask her about Sister Freweini but changed my mind in case I also endangered her life.

One day, the replacement nurse came as usual to check my health. She called me by name and said, "Aster, we have given you all the medical care we can at this hospital. To be honest, your medical problems demand better medical care. However, the hospital has its limits. In addition, we have been ordered by a higher authority that you ought to be discharged and returned to your place in Wia. So please be aware that you will leave the hospital in three days' time."

I stayed in the hospital for those few days. However, my illness and pain didn't show any signs of abating. In fact, my health deteriorated. I had no choice but to wait in faith for God's mercy. I took courage and asked the nurse, "For four days I haven't seen Sister Freweini, who treated me before you, for four days. Has she taken a leave of absence?"

"No," she replied, "Though I don't know the reason, she, poor woman, is in prison with her baby."

I knew she was in trouble. If she hadn't been in prison, she would have visited me. I began to think about whether my mother and sister had arrived safely in Asmara or whether they had been arrested before they left Massawa.

Though it was not good, at least I had found some information about Sister Freweini, but there was nobody from whom I could get information about my mother and sister.

One mid-morning, the soldier who gave me a visit with the two undercover security agents returned along with another soldier and entered my room.

"I hope the nurse has informed you. Since you have received appropriate medical care and your health has improved, you will have to return to your quarters. Pack your things. If there are forms to fill, we will inform the doctor and his assistants. Make sure to fill them. We will be back tomorrow." And they left. I began psychological preparations to return to Wia, the place I had suffered for years.

On that day, I decided to read my father's letter. I tore the envelope open after a lot of struggle and tears. I took out the letter and began reading it. I felt worried in case the tears that flowed destroyed Father's beautiful and well-crafted handwriting. The letter read thus:

"The daughter I love from the bottom of my heart, and the daughter whom I see but cannot have enough of. My beloved, above everyone, sweet, and dear daughter. I won't ask how you are. I know in what kind of place you are in and the situation you are in. I don't need to ask. I pray that God would lay His right hand on you."

"Let alone for years, I didn't want you to live away from me even for a second. Now that I haven't seen you for years, I miss you a lot. And your love always causes me a lot of suffering in my heart. Since I am a father, I have found it hard to bear. Even though I have tried, I have been unable to bear it."

"The day I heard about the news of your incarceration I can never forget: It has left a black scar and pain I cannot erase off my mind. I was unable to do anything. Due to extreme grief, as I returned home from work, I wandered off the sidewalk, and a car hit me. God lightened my injury, but I took medical leave from work and had to stay at home."

"I often wondered and got enraged asking myself, 'Why didn't my beloved daughter keep her faith in her heart and get on with her business?'"

"Your dream was to please God and to help human beings. For this reason, you tried very hard to achieve the highest in your academic efforts. I was very proud, especially after I came to know about your Matriculation grades. I know these people who have incarcerated you. I know that the violence they unleash would be harsh, for I know that they are shameful and defiled."

"Later, however, I remembered that I often told you this proverb: 'Man should pay his life for what he believes in.' Though as a parent I felt grieved, I was proud of your determination and your bravery. I think they would have been fortunate if they had realized that the determination and intelligence you demonstrated does not make you a criminal, but your contributions to society would have been tremendous and this was a loss to the country."

"I have left no stone unturned just to see you in the flesh. However, I have not succeeded. I asked my brother, Colonel Berhane, for help. However, he gave me no good reason but flimsy ones and words of arrogance. He had no other words for me. It is inevitable that we will meet one day, at the time God wills."

"The young man who used to accompany you to school came home and comforted me. He didn't leave my side as you wouldn't. But he himself met the same fate. They came and took him away from his home and there is no word about him up to this point. His poor grandmother who raised him is bedridden from her grief."

"My dear sweet and beloved daughter, this world is a place of test. People do not succeed unless they are tested. Therefore, when you are tested at your tender age, it shows that God has prepared something great for you. Don't be discouraged. Be strong! Be steadfast! May God who passed through and rescued the friends of Daniel from the blazing fire also rescue you from fire!"

"Beloved daughter, you are always in my heart and in my

prayers. God be with you. From the father that loves you and desires to see you even for just a minute."

After I read the letter, I wept the whole day and night inconsolably. Homesick and lonely, I prayed thus: "O Lord, if I have come to the end of my journey, please take me home to my father."

Because I realized the letter might cause my family more trouble. I reluctantly tore it to pieces. I had no reason why I should keep it. Sooner or later, they would find it. I couldn't hide it from them.

In the morning, the two soldiers came. "Let's go!" They hustled me. Still in my hospital clothes, I followed them slowly. They put me in a covered car and started driving like the wind.

25

Sister Freweini in Wia

The two soldiers filled the car with the smoke from their cigarettes. I felt troubled. In a soft voice I pleaded with them, "Can we have a break? Please?" They, however, didn't care about me.

After a few minutes, they stopped the car, left me inside, and went out either for toilet time or to have a bite.

As a matter of fact, they shouldn't have left me in the car alone. But, I think the reason they left me in the car was that they decided I was too weak to run away. To be honest, if I had the strength and energy, I think I would have escaped. But, in the situation I was in, that was impossible. They had closed the window and it was very hot. I was about to pass out.

An hour later, they came back talking and laughing about the food they ate and the drinks they had. On my part, I had taken nothing save the cup of tea I had when I left the hospital. As they talked, my mouth began to water.

One of them asked me in a jeering tone, "Do you have a boyfriend?"

His question irritated me, and I grinned. The second man said, "They have innumerable friends. They don't feel any shame. They do all kinds of things in the open."

They continued calling me names to humiliate me.

"You would be surprised," one of them said, "They claim that they have prayer meetings. They turn off the light, and the men and the women commit a lot of shameful things. May God destroy them!"

He showered obscenities on me.

"Do you know?" he addressed me, "In the house of one of the people you claim as your leader, they found thousands of US dollars."

Let alone bothering to answer him, if I could, I would have blocked my ears.

The second one said, "I am amazed. Even Orthodox priests and church ministers are affected by such a plague. Our government, however, has taken good care of them!"

They falsely accused and tainted the names of the priests and church ministers who were in prison at that time. My ears were forced to hear their vulgarities while my nose breathed in the smoke of their cigarettes.

In pain and suffering, I arrived in Wia.

I had no strength to get out of the car. They called some people and ordered them to carry me to some designated place. The people dumped me there where three or four other people were staying and left.

The sisters saw me, and they were shocked out of their wits. I hovered between life and death, and they did everything they could to help. They gave me the usual 'remedy' – *tihni.* I slowly began to regain my strength. Since it was late at night, I slept like a log.

The next morning I woke up more invigorated. I heard a voice I knew well. I carefully checked to be sure I was not dreaming. I wasn't. She came and hugged me tightly.

"Good morning!" she said. "Yesterday, you arrived very late at night, and you didn't know your surroundings well so you didn't recognize me."

I was unable to control my tears. Neither was I able to speak. For about half an hour, I refused to be comforted. Later, however, they calmed me, and I stopped weeping.

It was Sister Freweini, the nurse from the hospital in Massawa. I was surprised by the speed at which they brought her here. I had no doubt that Sister Freweini was here because of her connections with me so I very much wanted to hear her story. The most surprising thing was that I could read no signs of sadness on her face whatever. On the contrary, her face shone as the anointed morning sun.

Sister Freweini was brought here, to this place of suffering and disgrace, forced to leave sick children and her family behind. However, we could see that God had kept her heart unshaken. Her demeanor was a testimony to all.

"When did you come here?" I asked her softly.

She smiled and said, "I have been here a week now."

"How quickly they brought here!"

"Maybe God wants me to meet you!" she answered me.

I asked her to tell me everything she knew about what happened.

She told me her story.

"The hospital administration knows I am a Christian. And because of my faith, I have borne a lot of miseries. It is not new that I am here. One day, I was incarcerated when I was five months pregnant because I was found in a prayer meeting with other Christians. My health was not that good at that time, so they released me one month before delivery. At another time, we had a Bible study at my home. A policeman, my neighbor, used to watch our activities. Later, some policemen came and arrested my husband and me."

"They forced me into a car, and I fell down. My leg broke. I was also two months pregnant. As the result I had a miscarriage. So you see, I am used to suffering."

She continued, "When you were admitted to the hospital and when I was treating you, a nurse was watching my actions."

I interrupted her, "Is she dark-coloured and short haired?"

"Yes," she answered me.

"But it was she who told me about your incarceration."

"God forgive her," she said. "It was she who reported to the security people my relationship with you and that I contacted your family and arranged the reunion. She met me when I took your mother and sister to the road. The next morning, security came and took us all to the police station.

I interrupted her with my sobs, "And now, my mother and my sister?"

She said, "Please, let me finish!" She rebuked me. "They then questioned us. They especially quizzed your mother and sister. Finally, they intimidated both of them and ordered them to leave Massawa immediately. But they told me that I had to stay in the police station for the night. I told them that my children had nobody to look after them. But nobody cared or listened. You see, my youngest son cannot sleep without me. Three days later, they brought me here before I could make sure that my children would be safe."

"She is receiving all this suffering because of me," I thought, saddened. "It would have been better if I had not gone there, and I had died here." The nurse comforted me, "Don't be discouraged! All this is happening because God has prepared something valuable for us!" We hugged each other and cried in each other's embrace. We especially prayed that God would take care of her very young children.

My health began to deteriorate again. Sister Freweini took care of me, taking advantage of her knowledge even though she had no medical supplies or other necessities.

One day, a soldier came and told me that I was wanted in the office and ordered me to go with him.

"How can I go to the office? Even to the toilet, I go with the support of others. I can not walk to the office."

Angry, he told me that he didn't care and that was not his problem. I refused to go. I saw him change into a tiger. Enraged, he approached me pulling me by the hair and dragging me out of my bed. My hair was pulled out and I saw it in his hand.

Shocked, the soldier threw my hair toward me and went outside. The women in the room with me began to shriek and scream. I had very long hair. I was known in my neighboured as "the long-haired girl." But now most of my hair was gone. And what had been left had been pulled out. However, I was willing to sacrifice not only my hair but my everything.

The next morning, the soldier came back again and said, "Let's go!" Now, I knew it was useless to argue with him so I gathered all my strength and started walking. However, unable to do so, I collapsed.

Enraged, he called me names and insulted me, "You are a lying cheat! A fraud!"

The nurse boldly told him, "Aren't we your sisters? How can you be so cruel to us?"

He hit her until she vomited blood. The previous day, he pulled out my hair and now he had beaten her almost dead. Then he left.

The next day, he came with another soldier. As I asked myself what he was going to do, he stood like a statue before me.

26

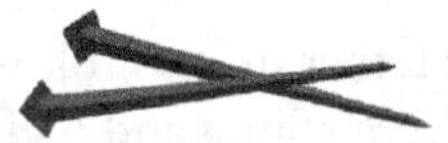

Sister Freweini's Serious Illness

Sister Freweini was still groaning in pain from the beating she received for speaking up for me. She shook the place with her screams for her pain was so great. The soldier who stood before us didn't care and he firmly ordered us to stand up and start moving.

I was unable to control my anger and in a rage declared, "Do whatever you will! Nothing will move us from this place!" Enraged, he left after calling us names.

The nurse endured a lot of pain for about a week as well as suffering as a mother missing her children. You see, as time passes you begin to see such events as normal. Sister Freweini, like us, got used to the suffering and distress.

After a few days, a soldier came and told us to get ready since we are going to leave this pace shortly then he immediately left. We had taken moving from place to place as a normal routine of imprisoned life. So we didn't respond immediatly. God gave us time to talk about many things, as talking was a therapy for us.

Sister Freweini had suffered much just because she was a Christian. She was from a well-to-do family and had endured great pressure from her own family members also. She particularly bore great suffering when she decided to marry the man who was now the father of her children. They had known each other since they were young and had ministered in church together for a long time. They loved each other. However, when they decided to get married, her family didn't accept the union. The family was approached by the elders to give their consent, but they refused. Later, she was told either to marry another man or leave her family home. Because she loved this Christian man she decided to marry him and was thus expelled from her family's home. Her wedding expenses were paid for by the church and by some generous Christian brothers and sisters. She led a good life until her husband had undertake National Service.

After her husband went into National Service, many complications began to emerge in her life. Particularly, a colonel was bothering here even though he knew she was married. He and his associates inflicted a lot of suffering on her husband. The colonel came drunk, banged on her door, intimidated her and threatened to rape and kill her. After sometime, however, he was transferred to another place and she got some peace.

In Wia, Sister Freweini never stopped thinking about her husband and children. She wept bitterly, especially when she thought of her youngest son. She repeatedly asked the authorities about his situation but they gave her no answer except, "You tell us the secrets you know!" Or "You sign this paper renouncing your faith!" They gave her no resolution to her requests. Her problem was a burden for me too. Added to my physical suffering, I had no peace of mind about what she was undergoing.

Three months passed since the order for us to move to another place was given. Due to the excessive anxiety about her children and her intense pain, Sister Freweini developed depression. She talked about nothing but her children the whole day and night. There was no way we could help her except pray for her and weep with her.

After six months in Wia, the extreme anxiety caused her to lose her mind. However, there was nothing that could be done even for such a very difficult situation. My friends and I prayed and wept for her constantly. A soldier came two or three times a day and intimidated and threatened me, "You too will go mad like her!"

One day, I was sitting in the blazing heat. I prayed and sobbed uncontrollably, "O God! If you really love me, please take me home and let me rest. I can't go beyond this point." At that time, I heard a loud voice, "You will declare the glory of God! You will not die!"

I answered half-angrily, "What is left of me? I am already dead!" Once more, the voice said, "I am the God of all flesh! Is there anything impossible for me?" After that, perfect peace began to flow into my heart.

"You aimless wanderer! Stand up and go away!" If the voice of the soldier hadn't brought me to reality, I think I would have lingered there to continue to hear God's voice.

Sister Freweini's condition worsened. She screamed and sobbed endlesslely day and night. Consequantly we spent our days and nights without a wink of sleep. She had been incarcerated in

Wia for one year now. Her only crime was helping 'a criminal' like me, and above all, for being a believer. Who wouldn't be anxious and go mad being a mother and wondering whether your children had anyone to look after them while you spent all your days in prison unable to intervene.

By the grace of God, enduring my pain and suffering, I was able to give Sister Freweini some moral and spiritual support. The support I gave her was not hidden from our tormentors, the soldiers who mistreated us. To break our morale, they separated me from her even though she had developed extreme anxiety. They locked me in an underground dungeon for several months.

These were the worst days of my suffering and distress. I am used to such punishment. However, I was unable to bear the separation from my sister who was in such extreme anxiety and suffering. I spent my days and nights alone, screaming and sobbing.

One day, a soldier brought me a cup of tea and a loaf of bread. In a weak voice, I begged him, "Please, take me to the nurse. Or at least bring me word about her."

I saw the soldier's face flood with tears. He was unable to control his feelings. He lifted me from the floor and told me, "Don't lose heart! I will do my best!" He wiped his tears and disappeared from my sight swiftly, lest they find out that he was seen with me.

Not every soldier was cruel.

Two weeks later, they returned me to my place. Sister Freweini hugged me tightly when she saw me. Uttering her husband's and her children's names, she asked me, "Have you found them? Have you brought them?"

At this time, I began to cry bitterly like a new born baby who has just come out of his mother's womb. The nurse wailed, "Have they taken him? Have they killed him? O my children!"

She wept with me. O how compassionate is the heart of a mother! My mother is worrying about me in just such a way. Grief killed my father because he loved me this way.

"It is tough to be a parent!" I said in my heart.

Sister Freweini's condition deteriorated by the day. She began to spurn the food and ate just enough to keep body and soul together. She was now only a pack of bones. Her beautiful countenance fell. There was a difference of worlds between the nurse I saw in the hospital and this pack of bones. However, there was a hymn she sang loudly when she was in difficult situations. The hymn was, "You are good, God! Goodness is Your nature and attribute, God!"

Probably, it appears to some of you as foolishness to sing such hymns in such a situation. However, we felt the presence of God through all our hardship.

Two years had passed since the order to move was given. The order was forgotten. By the grace of God, slowly, Sister Freweini began to return to consciousness and normality.

One day, early in the morning, some soldiers came and said, "Hurry up! Hurry up! Pack quickly!" They then shoved me, Sister Freweini, and two other Christians into a car before driving off at high speed. Uninformed about the destination of the trip, we continued the journey wondering.

27

In Mietir

The car we were travelling in was filled with cigarette smoke. I felt overwhelmed so I begged, “Could you please open the window?”

The two men, however, acted as if they had not heard my request. Not only were they smoking, but they also chewed tobacco. So, they filled the car with the tobacco they spat out.

Sister Freweini begged them in tears, “Where are we going? Please, take me where my children are. They have nobody but me.”

One of the soldiers grinned and mocked her, “If you loved your children, you wouldn’t have gotten involved in such a religion illegitimized by the government and the people, a religion that is an instrument of the CIA. Now, stop shedding hypocritical tears!”

She sobbed uncontrollably turning the car into a place of

mourning. The soldier was unable to bear her tears. He threatened her, "One more sound, I will throw you out in the desert, and you would be food for wild animals."

I knew we were already in the midst of wild animals. Therefore, I prayed to God so that He might give her peace. I put my hand on her head and in a soft voice, I told her, "Don't be discouraged! God is not dead!"

I repeated this three times.

As soon as the soldiers heard the word "God," they started laughing loudly together. One of them said, "Did you say, 'God is not dead'? If there was a God, how is it that he can't get you out of your suffering? Now, know this: We are the gods and rulers of this country! Now, God is an image that you created in your head. There is no God!"

I didn't think it was fruitful to engage in a discussion. In addition, because we had no food or drink, our strength had gone, and we were completely exhausted.

After a long drive, we arrived at a place surrounded by mountains. In my heart, I said, "Wia is a very big place." I was unable to distinguish this place from where we had been. Due to the intense heat I must have been deluded and thought, "They just want to put pressure on us. They have taken us around a very long distance but have brought us back to where we were."

Countless people moved here and there. I realized that a great number of people were incarcerated.

One of the soldiers asked us, "Do you know where you are?" Sister Freweini, completely exhausted, didn't say a word.

I answered him, "Where can you take us except Wia?"

The soldiered jeeringly said, "This place is much worse than where you were. Here you will drink the cup of suffering to the fullest. This place is called Mietir." [Mietir, or Me'eter prison, is situated along the Red Sea coast between Karora and Massawa, north of the capital Asmara. The prison houses a large number of prisoners of conscience and other political prisoners].

Even though we had started drinking the cup of suffering a long time ago, and we took it as a normal part of our life, I knew in my heart that this place would be worse than Wia.

This place differed from Wia because it had elderly people, men and women, as prisoners. They dumped Sister Freweini and me in a place where there were many young women.

When they saw us, the women were filled with compassion and did everything in their power to make us feel comfortable. They brought us food to eat and something to drink. However, we were unable to eat because we were beyond hungry. We ate a little and went to bed.

The next morning, I was struck with surprise by the things I saw. I was particularly shocked when I saw a Christian woman in a wheel chair. Her name was Rigat.

Rigat addressed me, "Good morning! How was the journey? Are you still tired?"

She smiled at me.

It was very hard to harmoniously reconcile the situation she was in and the smile on her face. I slowly went to her and told her my name. She replied that her name was Rigat, and we had a chat for a few minutes.

I came to know that she was in her thirties and was disabled due to polio that attacked her during her childhood. She was in

Mietir after she was arrested and brought there because of her faith. I knew that God had many heroes and heroines of faith, and I thanked Him.

It was obvious that even a healthy person would face a lot of challenges and problems in Mietir, let alone a disabled person.

I asked her how long she had been in Mietir. "Almost a year," she answered.

I informed her that I came from Wia where I was incarcerated for more than six years and that through my distress and sufferings, I would glorify God with my life. She wept for joy and comforted me, "We must go through hardships to enter the kingdom of God."

Rigat was a church minister who had actively ministered in one of Eritrea's regions. However, one day, the security forces brought her and her friends to Mietir. She told me about the tortures and beatings carried out in this place.

The stories she told me didn't surprise me for I had similar experiences, and they were not new. However, when she told me how they tortured another disabled sister whose name was Simret, to be honest, I wept bitterly. Simret was arrested when she and other Christians were praying in a New Year meeting.

At midnight, the police came and surrounded them. The police arrested everyone including Simret and brought to Mietir. With her extreme disability in one foot, Simret was in intense pain ever since.

"One day," Rigat told me, "They took Simret somewhere and beat her very severely. A National Service soldier assigned there deliberately took a stick and beat her on both the injured and the good leg, until they both began to bleed. As he beat her, he asked, 'Why did you forsake the religion of your forefathers? Why did you follow a faith that is against the country?'

"He brought a lot of suffering and pain on Simret beating her until she became unconscious. However, she answered him, 'I won't deny Jesus. Not now, not in the future!'

"Finally, after sometime, they released her, in case she died in their custody."

Rigat told me, "Here, there is not a single kind of suffering that has not been carried out, only one that have not been reported"

Rigat and I had a good time together for a while.

Sister Freweini's condition deteriorated. Her problem was known among many brothers and sisters who prayed for her and comforted her.

One afternoon a soldier came and took me to an office where the soldier there questioned me, "Why did you choose to suffer? Why don't you admit your wrongdoing and get your freedom?"

I had heard such talk for years and so disregarded it. But he added words that cut to my heart, "Your father died before you had an opportunity to see him. Your brother is suffering in Alaa. No one knows if you will see your mother after sometime."

I asked him, "What is wrong with my mother?"

He laughed, "It is for this reason that we urged you to admit your wrongdoing!"

I realized that something must be wrong with my mother. In

my heart, I said, "O God, my father is with you. And now, is my mother going to die before I see her?"

Tears began to flow from my eyes. The soldier, unable to bear my tears, ordered me, "Out of my office! But, before you leave – remember, starting from tomorrow you must come here everymorning to sweep this place and make us breakfast. You will be told your remaining duties tomorrow."

I remembered Rigat's words, "Here everyone is a slave, and they are the masters."

The only things that made Mietir different from Wia was that in the former you were always a slave serving the officers and the soldiers.

I began to cry thinking of my mother and the forced assignment I had been given and returned to my place. When I arrived, I found all of my sisters weeping and wailing with bowed heads. I thought they must have had the same experience as mine, and I began to weep and wail with them.

I heard one of the sisters say, "I saw him from a distance only last week. Poor man, the good thing is that he has gone to be with the Lord!"

I asked the sister closer to me what had happened. She answered me, "There was an old man among those incarcerated here last year. The man was old, and he had poor health. He fell very ill right from the time he came from Asmara till he went to be with the Lord! In addition, he bore a lot of punishment, and the heat gave him much trouble. He had asked to get medical attention, but he got no answer. Today he didn't get up from his bed and was found dead."

I was very saddened.

"Now, have they sent his body to Asmara?" I asked her.

She told me, "According to a brother who works here, they have sent word they are sending his body to his family."

I knew that our tormentors were cruel and possessed by an evil spirit. Our souls suffered the whole night from the sad news as well as the terrible heat.

The next morning, I reluctantly started walking to the commander's home to carry out the duties that I was assigned.

28

An Incident Claims Innocent Lives

Mietir is different from Wia in that there is no work here – day or night. Sometimes work is good because, though exhausting, it keeps you busy. In Mietir, at least you needed to have something to read so that the weather and the dark thoughts in your mind did not cause a lot of anxiety.

One of the methods of punishment they use is to let your mind idle without work to allow dark thoughts torment you. This is to encourage you to do something desperate. In this place, there are innumerable young people who could be of service to the country. You can easily see how the country is being destroyed.

I started to walk to the official's residence to carry out the duties given to me. The house was very far away from where we lived. Exhausted, I collapsed half way.

Some people who saw me from afar came running and asked me if I am ok.

I told them that I was very tired.

"Where are you going in such intense heat?" they asked me. I explained.

One young man asked me, "Are you a believer?"

I told him that I was. It looked as if he knew the situation well and that he had a good knowledge of what was happening.

"Don't be afraid. We are your fellow Christians." They gave me something to eat and drink from what was in their hand. I regained some of my strength.

"Let me go," I told them and stood up to go.

"No," they said. "You can't go. How can you, as you are? It is impossible." They tried to dissuade me from going.

I fearfully told them, "Dear brothers, I have been incarcerated for the Lord for years. I know these people! They are cruel beasts! They will punish me! To be honest, all my strength is gone. Any punishment I receive now will spell my death. Therefore, let me go. I will walk slowly."

I tried to persuade them to let me go.

They told me, "Dear sister, we know the road. You will die before you reach there. You may be surprised to know the officials don't call young women to make them coffee. They have their own servants. Knowing your condition, it is their trick to start you out so that you faint on the way and die on the road. Now, don't you worry. We will find a way."

So, they took me to their place.

It was very dangerous to carry out Christian activities in Mietir. However, Mietir is a place surrounded by mountains, and you could pray and read the Bible behind one of the mountains. Unconscious of time, I spent long hours with the brothers.

I set off on the way home before the soldiers on guard duty came out. As I left their place, about five brothers came running and said, "Brothers, be stout hearted! God is with you. We were informed that our term had come to an end, and we will start going home this week."

They told us the good news.

To be honest, in my heart I prayed, "God, when is my time?" I didn't want to miss this opportunity. I gave them the address of my house in Asmara and earnestly asked them to find out about my family.

When I returned to my place, I began to worry because I hadn't gone to the official's home. I spent a sleepless night worrying whether they would come and take me.

When a week passed, I remembered the brother's words. He had told me, "You see, if they have thrown you here, in this place of suffering like a useless household item, they don't remember you."

Enduring the heat of Mietir the whole day without work and sitting idly, I took as part of my life. One day, about mid-morning, I saw the brother I met on the road coming toward me, and I was overjoyed. It was because I thought that he had brought me news and word of my family. As he came closer, my heart began to beat much faster. I began to pray so that my heart would calm down. He called me by name and gave me a warm greeting.

"I was sent on an errand" he told me, "But, when I saw you from a distance, I decided to talk to you for a few minutes."

“You have done the right thing,” I told him. “How are you?”

“I am fine,” he answered me. “But the accident that happened to our brothers broke my heart!”

Inadvertently, he broke the sad news to me.

“Which brothers?” I asked, shocked.

“The brothers who finished their term and said goodbye last time.”

“What about them?” I asked him, pressing him to answer me. “What happened to them? Were they told that they can’t go home again?”

“It would have been much better if they had told them they were not going home,” he told me in tears. “As they were going home, some brothers fell off the pick up truck in which they were travelling. Three were killed, and most of the rest of them were seriously injured. The pickup truck was moving very fast, and they were riding in the back.”

I was stunned. Some of these brothers who thought their suffering had come to an end, some of them had met their cruel end while others became disabled.

I was furious. “Why didn’t they take them in a covered truck? And this in such a hot weather. O God of Abraham, Isaac, and Jacob, when are you going to deal with their intimidation?”

I prayed in intense bitterness.

I expected to hear news of my family but, instead, what I was hearing was the bad news of the death and injury of these brothers. I cried my heart out.

The brother told me not to weep. “The dead have gone to the

Lord. As to the injured, may the hand of the Lord be with them!" He continued, "This week is a terrible week. Last Monday and Tuesday, we buried two brothers."

Death, suffering, and bitterness had become our lot. These had become daily realities. We were leading very difficult and bitter lives. However, I had no doubt that our reward from the Lord of love would be great.

How would their parents (who expected their arrival) take it when the news of their death was broken to them? Though death for us was an everyday occurrence, to accept the death of these brothers whose lives were snuffed out at a tender age and were going home at the end of their term, was very hard.

Sister Freweini saw me weeping and said, "Have my children died? My son (mentioning his name) got drowned in Gurgusum [a beach in Massawa]? And they have killed my husband?"

She continued asking these questions. She always, day and night, talked about her children and her husband. The soldiers intentionally made her situation worse so that her condition would deteriorate. Her condition became a more unbearable burden than the sufferings I underwent.

In the area where I was assigned, we had three women aged above fifty. They were arrested at three different events in different places and were brought here to this camp. I thought one of the women looked an exact copy of my mother, and so when I saw her, I was filled with inexpressible feelings. I tried to have a chat with her. However, I was unable to do so.

One day, however, God gave me an opportunity, and I had a chance to talk to her. When I told her about myself, one of the women took a netsela and began wailing in great sadness.

Fearing worse could befall us, the two women rebuked the third, and the woman controlled her tears. Sorry for her that she had to be here at such a delicate age, I asked her to tell me her story.

The three women had similar stories. The third woman, Weizero [Mrs] Rigbe, however, had a sixteen year old son incarcerated with her in Mietir. Though she had asked the officials to be able to see her son in the same prison camp, she told us that she had been denied permission.

One of the women told me, "My daughter, I am not only your mother, I am your grandmother too. I am here in my fifth month. But I am not afraid and have no worry for Jesus is with me. Surely you also a very young girl, have experienced terrible sufferings? But let's not lose heart, Jesus is with us."

She comforted us with her words. She continued, "This is the third time I have been imprisoned. One day, I was also imprisoned at the Fifth Station with my children. But I was released a month later. Another time, I was charged with the crime of conducting Christian meetings during night hours and I was taken away from home and imprisoned for three months at Mai Temenai. You see, it has become our second nature to suffer for the Lord."

She told us her story with a smile on her face.

It was late at night. Fearing that the guards would catch us red-handed chatting, we quietly went to our places. The faith and confidence of the mothers greatly strengthened my faith.

Three days later, I met the brother who had broken the bad news. I asked him if he had any news about the injured brothers. He informed me that one of them had died before he reached the hospital but that the others were receiving medical care. He was in a hurry and told me, “Secretly, I will come this week, and we will have a chat.”

He left immediately.

Saddened by the news and in deep thought, I went to my place and sat down.

29

An Amazing Revelation

Days were replaced by weeks and months by years. Many years had passed since I left home. Seen through natural eyes, the years I spent in prison for the sake of the Lord were wasted years. I knew full well what level and position I would have achieved in those lost years. Especially, in times of suffering and distress, and in some particular places and situations, Satan used all kinds of arrows and traps to attack my mind.

I am a human being, and because weakness is part of my nature, often the question 'Why?' filled my mind. Sometimes criminals and violent people and the unjust have plenty and enjoy life, while the likes of me (who committed no crime or did no wrong but hold fast to our own faith) are beaten, suffer, or die. This raises a tough question of 'Why?' But I had no doubt that the suffering we experienced would be repaid with glory.

One day, about three or four of us incarcerated for our faith, had a chat. Sitting idle the whole day without any work bores one very much. Hence, when there was an opportunity, we held a discussion. In this chat, I heard an amazing testimony of a Christian sister.

This sister started her testimony with a question. She asked us, "Do you remember when Bibles were burned at Enda Silassie, Enda Medhanie Alem, and Enda Mariam Churches?" Every one of us nodded our heads, telling her that we remembered the incident.

"At that time, I didn't go to church. I didn't pray, and I had disgraceful life," she continued. "We had a neighbor, my mother's friend, who had the ear of the administration. At the same time, she was a relative of my mother. She used to tell us bad things about Christians. She said that Christians corrupted the Coptic Orthodox faith that they rose against the government, preaching it was wrong to fight, and handed over the country to the Woyane [Ethiopian regime]. When you hear such things, you are incited against them in hatred, and such hatred has no comparison. My brother, especially, was very incensed."

"One day, our neighbour came to visit us, and she was drinking coffee with my mother. She smiled and said, 'Now, our government has devised a wonderful plan against these pork-eaters. Promise you won't tell this. Yesterday, there was a meeting in the local administration. Enraged, a colonel angrily told us, 'The solution is in your hand. Why have you not taken any action up to now?' You will hear some good news this week. We will send fire into their midst.'"

"Amazed, my mother asked, 'What are you going to do to them?'"

"She answered, 'May the kind government live forever! The

government has given us information on how to go about it.'"

"About one week later, she called my brother and me. In her house were about three or four young men from our neighbourhood and other young people from other areas. After we had a very delicious lunch, she brought us together. 'Children,' she addressed us. 'Tomorrow, together we will uproot these corruptors of our faith who disturb the church. We will burn their disreputable book and damage their property. We will make sure that they do not return to the church a second time.'"

"To be honest, I was very frightened, and so I asked her, 'How about if the government imprisoned us?' Two other people also asked similar questions. She smiled and said, 'Don't you worry about that! Do you think the government likes them? Don't be foolish! Do you think we will do this without the consent of the government?' Every one of us went home, feeling reassured."

"The next day, the other people and I went to Enda Mariam Church and turned it upside down. The government had secretly supported our action, and so when people complained about the infringement of their rights, nobody gave them an ear. Later, when I believed in Christ, my brother told me that he and his friends threw condoms into Enda Medhanie Alem Church. Later, they told other people that they found the condoms in the church and spread the news throughout Asmara." She told us this amazing story.

In the middle of our chat, one sister came screaming and weeping, "Help! Help! Please, help!"

We ran with her without knowing what had happened. We found Sister Freweini outstretched and unconscious. She lived in Massawa and was no stranger to hot places. But now, distress, hunger and longing for her children took a toll on her and brought her down.

Here, nobody's cries were heard, and the distress of everyone was ignored. We asked for help. However, there was no one who cared to help. After many hours, some people came to give first aid.

Her condition was that she missed her children and her family. Since this problem caused her great sadness, it led to anxiety. The people who came to give her medical help told us that she had passed away. I collapsed where I was.

Her husband and children would not leave my mind. I could not weep for my eyes had gone dry. I was unable to scream for I had no strength left. I could not cry because I had lost hope. I became like a lifeless statue. I didn't know how long I stayed there.

I regained awareness of my surroundings when I heard a voice, "Sister, get up. It is already dawn. Get up. It is enough!"

After that, my tears began to flow unbidden. Without exaggeration, I kept weeping almost the whole day until it was dark. My heart was broken. Sister Freweini gave up her life for the sake of her faith and not to deny the Lord, who loved her. She didn't have enough time with her children. She didn't enjoy the embrace and love of her husband. She went to the Lord, remembering and calling the names of her children and her husband day and night. Her husband was unable to look after their children, for he was serving in the endless National Service. He had heard of the imprisonment of his wife, and it was obvious that he had asked for leave.

Sadness and grief filled my heart.

As I was in my broken state, a sister checking the clothes of

Sister Freweini and found an envelope with my name on it.

She came to me and said, "I think this letter is for you." My hands began to shake as I tried to open it, and my heart began to pound in my chest. I prayed to God in my heart. After I began to read the letter tears flowed down my cheeks.

"The sister I love, a hero of the Faith, and valiant in the Lord, Dear Sister, I miss my children terribly. I miss my husband. But above all, I miss the Lord and desire to see His face. I know that He also is waiting for me."

"Don't be discouraged. The sufferings you have borne are not without rewards. A crown of life is ready for you. But, I will go and see Him first. Dear sister, if God has given you an opportunity and you are released, please kiss my children for me. Hug them and tell them how much I love them. They are God's gift to me. Do you appreciate how much I love them? And tell my kind husband that I have gone to the Lord having finished the race and having kept the faith. Tell him also that I have loved him to the end. And tell my parents that I have been very faithful and loved the Lord a lot. God bless you."

That was the content of the letter.

The most amazing thing was that the letter was written a week before her death. She was certain that she would sleep in death. The letter she wrote me tremendously increased the faith I had in the Lord.

Even as we were in this state of mind for two weeks, we continuously got engaged in activities and tasks that exhausted us. Here our labour was free. They used it as they wanted. It especially broke one's heart to see highly educated brothers engaging in such menial labour.

For three months, I tried to find people who would deliver the letter Sister Freweini wrote to her loved ones and people who could get me news about my family.

At that time, I saw from a distance someone I knew very well.

30

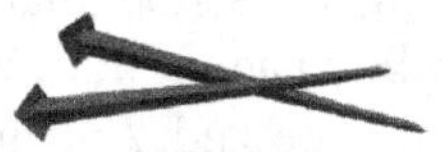

News about My Mother

When I saw Tedros from a distance, my heart began to beat wildly. I wanted to run and greet him, but he made a sign telling me not to come closer to him. Unable to do anything, I scanned my surroundings up and down, before and behind me. Once again, he made another signal and told me not to move from where I was.

He disappeared from sight in a moment. Hopeful, I stayed where I was for about half an hour. Later, however, I lost hope, and I prayed that God would give me another opportunity to meet him and started walking to my place.

After a few steps, I heard my name being called from behind. I turned back, jumped, and hugged Tedros. When he saw me, tears began to flow from his eyes. I knew I had changed so much, and I had lost weight considerably. I knew he was weeping because he saw the changes in my physical appearance. I also read in his face that he had great and deep compassion for me.

Tedros lived in my neighborhood. Though he was not related to me by blood, our parents came from the same village, and so our relationship was very close. He was one of the most handsome young men in the neighbourhood. I remember when we were very young, my school mates and girls in the neighbourhood liked talking about him. We laughed and joked, "I will marry him," one said. And another would say, "No, he is mine." Now, he had completely changed. Without exaggeration, he had become a skeleton and lost all his attraction.

"I had heard that you were incarcerated. About five years ago, your sister told me. However, I didn't know you were here." When I heard the phrase 'five years ago,' I immediately knew that he had no news about my family.

In turn, I asked him, "How long have you been here? When did you come? Are you assigned here?" I bombarded him with my questions.

He smiled at me, "Do you mean exiled? I am here because I am incarcerated." I saw the expression on his face change. So I asked no more questions, lest I add more grief to his discomfort.

He continued, "You see, a few years after I graduated from the university, I had an opportunity to pursue my masters in the United States. I asked to be released. The department I was working with in the Ministry of Defence allowed me to leave. But when I went to the Ministry of Defence, the authorities refused to release me. However, because I was determined to pursue higher education and make use of the scholarship awarded to me, I decided to cross the border to a neighboring country to apply for a US visa and go to the US. I was caught.

Now, I became prey in the hands of these predators, and here I am suffering." I saw his eyes form tears.

He continued. "When they caught me, they put me in a prison called 'Track B.' The physical and psychological sufferings I bore at that place are hard to describe. After about a year and a few weeks, they accused me of nonsense and of being involved in a political plot. Then they brought me here."

He had experienced all kinds of sufferings he told me, and so I felt sorry for him, but I was not surprised. I very much wanted to know about my family and so asked him, "How is your family?"

He kept quiet for sometime and then said, "My family is not doing well. My father is ok, but he has found it hard to bear my mother's grief."

I began to weep because I remembered my mother.

"Has your mother died?" I asked him.

"Yes. Already this is her third year. My imprisonment and the grief of my brother's death as he crossed the border was too much for her and killed her."

I felt sorrow enter my heart. I wept bitterly for a few minutes.

"Don't cry," he comforted me. "You can't go through all our problems crying over them." He continued, "Do you have any news about your family?"

I could see he was afraid.

"Brother, please do something! My father is dead, and I am dying to get news of my mother."

He didn't let me finish, "I know. Before I came here my father visited me in Track B."

"Please, do your best and help me get news about my family," I begged him.

"Last year, my brother wrote me a letter. He told me that there were no young men in the neighbourhood because they had all crossed the border. However, he informed me that the families were fine."

I could see that he wanted to tell me something but was afraid.

"Brother, I can feel in my heart that you want to tell me something. Please don't hide anything from me," I pressed him.

"There is nothing to hide. I have told you everything."

I didn't let him off the hook. I pressed harder.

He said, "You see, your mother is a little bit sick. If you can talk to the officials, beg them and convince them to let you go and at least see your mother and then come back."

"You see, a friend's mother was very ill, and he found someone who could speak on his behalf, and I heard that they let him go. I am not sure that they did let him go. But at least go and beg them!"

When I heard this, my heart nearly failed me. My knees went weak. In broad daylight, I felt the place had gone dark. My eyes popped out, and I was about to lose balance and collapse. He quickly realized what was happening and walked with me, supporting me home.

When I heard this news, I didn't get a wink of sleep for two days. Like a statue I didn't utter even a word. My heart was filled with thoughts of my family and anxiety for my mother.

Though I had suffered and endured distress for many years, I had not missed my family as much as at that time. My mind was filled with many questions. Satan attacked me and filled my mind with his voice, "For what do you suffer all this?" I very much wanted to die. The sisters around me, however, tirelessly prayed for me, and their prayers gave me strength.

After a week, I told the sisters that my mother was very ill and that I wanted to see her. Here, the lawmakers and decision-makers were a handful. And these were heartless people. If you wanted to get what you desire, you had to give them what they want. I was not ready for that.

One day, one of the sisters relayed information about my condition to a person in authority. She was informed my request will be brought to the attention of the commander. I began to count the days like a pregnant woman, as the saying goes, waiting for an answer.

After a month, I was told that the commander had heard about my request and that he would look into it shortly. Because time doesn't wait for anyone, six months passed without an answer to my request.

One day, I saw Tedros with two other people approaching from a distance. Immediately I imagined he was going to break the news of my mother's death and my heart began to beat very loudly. I began to tremble. For sometime, he didn't realize that I was waiting for them to get closer. When he saw me, he stopped for a few seconds, and to the surprise of the people walking with him, he turned around and disappeared from my sight. Though I called him by name, he flew away as if he had not heard me. Then, I realized that he was hiding something from me.

"Mother! Mother! ..." I sobbed loudly and went into my room

which was made of stick walls. The sisters joined me in loud wailing for they thought that I had received news of the death of my mother, whose illness I had told them about. The room was turned into a mourning house. Immediately, some soldiers came and, in military order, told us to get out of our room.

One soldier in particular got angry with us and shouted, "Aha! You have gone too far! You want to incite rebellion through your wailing and sobbing?" He punished us military style until we could bear it no more.

One of us told him, "Brother, you have misunderstood us. We don't want to rebel. It is only that this sister has lost her mother, and she received the news right now. Death and mourning is part of us, and we are grieving with her."

She told this to him fearfully.

The soldier was enraged and turned into a wild beast.

"Which one of you received the news of her mother's death?" He began to scream.

Sobbing and weeping, I told him, "It is I."

He told all the sisters to go to their room, but he told me to remain where I was.

"You disgraceful woman! Accursed *pente*! Who are you trying to cheat? You devised this plan of your mother's death so that you may have the compassion of the officials to be released. Know this, let alone your tricks, you who were born just yesterday, we also know the tricks of America, funding you and your likes! Now, answer me. Who gave you this news of your mother's death?"

He pressed me to answer the question.

I had no answer, and I was in trouble. I didn't know what I was going to say. The brother told me only about my mother's illness, not her death. From the fact that he didn't want to meet me, I concluded that she must have died. Hence I wept and screamed. Revealing Tedros' identity to the soldier would get him in to serious trouble. I kept quiet.

The soldier could not bear my silence, so he struck me on my back with the stick in his hand.

"Look!" He said, "Either you tell me the information or I will kill you here!"

I didn't want to hand over the brother to the authorities, and so I decided to bear the suffering on my own. I answered him, "I cried because I missed my mother and because I could not bear my mother's longing, and a voice told me that my mother was dead."

"You are a liar! And a cheat!" he told me. He asked me again, "Who told you the news? You tell me quickly!"

"I have nothing more to add. That is the truth," I stuck to my story.

"Look!" he threatened me, "You will see who I am. You cannot fool me with the tears of the fake news of your mother's or your grandmother's death. You will weep some more. You will see who I am. Go to your place!"

He turned away quickly.

My spirit was overwhelmed with grief, my heart with bitterness, and my body with exhaustion. I began to see my mother like a photo in front of my eyes. As I was in such bitterness, I heard a verse in a loud voice, "When anxiety was great within me, your consolation brought joy to my soul."

Immediately, I felt the peace of God flow into my heavy heart like cool water. The surprising thing was that, if the Jesus whom I love, for whose sake I am suffering, had not supported me when I gave up and lost all hope, it was unimaginable that I would have borne such suffering.

The sisters who were with me comforted me.

The next morning, the soldier returned accompanied by two other soldiers. "Where is the woman who was causing disruption yesterday with the fake death of her mother or her aunt?"

They escorted me away, as the soldier called me names, in his rage and fury.

31

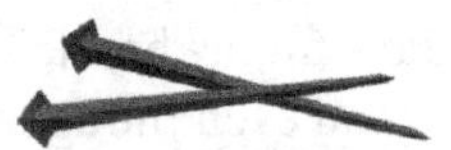

Remorseful Judas

One of the three soldiers took me away, calling me names. The other two, however, appeared unhappy, and said not a word. The abusive soldier ordered me to stay in the scorching sun. I sat on a small stone for about four hours until I could take it no more.

As I was so over wrought, I prayed to God in my heart to miraculously give me shade just as he grew a plant that gave the Prophet Jonah shade. In those four hours, more than the blazing sun and the extreme heat, it was Satan's flaming arrows (that he sent into my mind) that gravely wounded me.

Unconsciously, I prayed, "O God! Now, this has gone too long. How much longer am I to suffer?" Like Hagar in the desert not willing to watch the death of her son, I wept bitterly. In my spirit, a word came to me in a loud voice that said, "Be faithful, even to the point of death, and I will give you the crown of life."

I wiped my tears with my hands and boldly said, "O God, even if my sufferings increase and my cross becomes heavier, I will acknowledge your name and not deny it."

Immediately, Satan said in a voice in my mind, "Who are you talking with? With Someone you haven't seen? Why don't you deny all and enjoy the rest of your life?"

I felt a verse from the Bible fill my heart, "Though you have not seen him, you love him; and even though you do not see him now, you believe in him and are filled with an inexpressible and glorious joy, for you are receiving the goal of your faith, the salvation of your souls." So, I said loudly, "Amen."

A soldier called Habtom came closer to me and asked me, "Why are you talking to yourself? Come inside until the commander in charge arrives."

Habtom led me to a house much better than our thatched-roof house. There was nobody but us, and so I was very frightened. He knew I couldn't beat him if he tried to force me. If he tried to rape me, I decided to cry for help. He gave me water to drink and some bread. He looked me in the eye and wept and sobbed. I was confused.

I knew I was brought here for punishment, But when I saw him whom I suspected of harboring intentions of raping me weep, I could take it no more, and I too began to weep.

"You have nothing to weep about!" Habtom told me. "You should not weep. You are a hero who stood in her faith and a sister that suffering has not beaten. It is I who should weep. I am a Judas who has sold his Lord."

He wiped his tears away.

I realized that Habtom must have been a follower of Christ. "It is possible that I knew the Lord before you did. I served Him, sang to Him; I preached His gospel. But I was unable to stand in the faith. I loved the world like Demas. And now, I have become the persecutor of my brothers. Woe is me!"

He took a deep breath.

I didn't have much strength to speak, but I said, "Don't you know God gives the weak strength and to the feeble power? Didn't you read this in the Bible? Don't the people who have fallen down get up? And the weak, didn't they regain their strength?"

"You know what? I loved the Lord a lot, but I was unable to overcome the suffering that came my way. I am a married man. I love my wife very much. We had no children for a long time because it was God's will that way."

"One day, God heard our prayers and my wife became pregnant. We were overjoyed, and all the brothers and sisters who prayed for us thanked God."

"It was at about that time the church was shut down. My wife and I had a gathering to minister to, and we were praying and worshiping in one house, our meeting place."

"Suddenly, the police came and surrounded the house, and took us to prison. They took some of us to Sawa for forced National Service, and because my wife was pregnant, they took her by truck along with other elderly women to another place. My wife told me later that a soldier pushed her, and she felt her womb hurting a bit. Three days later, she miscarried. My wife was devastated and I was heartbroken."

"I came back home after I completed the military training. Some years later, my wife became pregnant again. She was probably seven or eight months pregnant. One day when I was ministering in a house someone informed the police came and arrested us."

"To be honest, I felt it deeply. In my heart, I told God that I was not ready for such suffering so I grumbled against Him. When my wife heard about it, she was shocked and her blood pressure rose, and she was taken to the hospital. The baby died in her womb. My sufferings were multiplied, and my wife became ill. My family pressed me to have a child. Reluctantly, I had a child by another woman out of wedlock. Now, my life is in a mess."

Such was the story of his bitter life. He added, "You see, suffering brings some closer to God, while it causes others to withdraw from Him."

I told him, "Remember those earlier days after you had received the light, when you stood your ground in a great contest in the face of suffering."

"I had a friend whom I cannot forget as long as I am alive," he told me. "You would be surprised to see this brother preaching the Bible eloquently. You never get tired of listening to him."

"You see, before I abandoned my faith, I had preached the Word. I only preached between forty minutes and one hour. I didn't like preaching or listening to someone longer than that time. When he preached, you could hear him even for ten hours, and you wouldn't get tired of listening to him. Especially, when he sang and when he led in worship, the heavens opened. God had blessed him both financially and in spiritual matters."

"However, when the church was closed, everything changed. This brother was very well known, and he was arrested like the others. He left his wife and his children and was sent to prison. However, prison was not good for him."

"As a matter of fact, despite prison, even when one is free, one cannot lead a decent life while these people are in charge. Later, these people wait until you are about to die. Did you think they cared about this brother when he was ill?"

"What is worse, I don't know what they told his wife. When I went to visit her, she sent someone to the door who informed me that she was out. If I saw her on the road, she would avoid me."

"Later, they sent him home when he was very ill. To my surprise, at this bitter hour his wife deserted him. What amazes me is not the suffering he endured. It is that he died without a word of complaint on his lips but full of songs of praise and thanksgiving."

"I don't know why God leaves the likes of me but takes such people home," he said and began to weep, bowing his head. "This brother always comes in my dreams and in my waking hours, and I feel that he tells me, 'Repent and get back to your God, to your ancient Rock.'"

He kept weeping.

He continued, "You would be surprised to hear this. After the Third Woyane Offensive, we used to hear and share the Word of God together with some Christians."

"One day, as a pure coincidence, the commander found us on his way to the toilet. They beat all of us until we had enough. They especially made it worse for our leader because they had targeted him before."

"After that, our brigade commander called a meeting. He made the brother stand in the midst of the whole brigade and told him, 'Now, I will see if you are a man.' He called him names and humiliated him. Then he said, 'I will burn you in the sight of everyone' and poured kerosene on the brother."

"The army began to grumble in fear. The brigade commander took out a lighter and tried to burn him. For about a minute everyone held their breath. It was as if heaven and earth also held their breath. Later, he kicked him. He gave the unit commander an order and left. This is the greatest miracle I have seen with my eyes."

To be honest, after the testimony I heard, I forgot my sufferings and pain, and my heart rejoiced in the faithfulness of the Lord as if I were only a child. I began to weep for joy. In the few minutes I had, I told the brother some words of comfort, and I boldly prayed for him, placing my hand on him."

The commander was about to arrive, and as though he were saying goodbye to me, Habtom told me, "The officer who has called you doesn't care about other things but only about satisfying his sexual desires. Therefore, don't let go of the Lord, for whose sake you have suffered those for years so that your years of suffering may not go in vain."

I had experienced such trials for years, and they had tempered me. I accepted his word of advice and vowed to stick to the Lord and renewed that vow yet again.

After sometime, a soldier came and took me to Colonel Haile's place.

"Listen," Colonel Haile addressed me, "Don't you feel a bit of shame? Or don't you understand? Or do you think we have CNN or Aljazeera here that you gather women and incite them?"

Colonel Haile mocked me. He continued, "Why weep for your mother? Don't you think it is wiser to pave the way for you to see your mother before she is dead?"

He continued, "You look like Mona Lisa, and very young at that. You suffer to such an extent and for a useless faith and let your beauty spoil. It is so amazing. You could have studied and earned your degree, and you could have been married, had children, and made a name for yourself. Alas! You wasted your opportunity. Alas! Alas! Alas! But even now you still have time."

He stretched his hand toward me.

I loudly said, "In the name of Christ Jesus, don't touch me! I am God's temple"

I screamed at the top of my voice.

"Go away! Go away!" he told me and slapped me hard till I fell down dizzy to the ground.

He kicked me with his foot once or twice until my back went numb. He called a soldier loudly and ordered him to take me out of the room. God willed it, and Habtom, the brother with whom I had a chat, supported me and led me out.

"Where are you taking her?" the Colonel asked him. Then he ordered him, "Leave her in the blazing sun!"

I was left in the sun until nightfall. Though extreme bitterness and pain overwhelmed me, I rejoiced in spirit in the Holy Spirit.

For the sake of the gospel we endured suffering and pain, hardship and injustice, hunger and thirst, beatings and death, and our hearts stayed fixed in the Lord. As the Apostle Peter said, it is not a defeat but a victory to endure suffering as a Christian. It is a blessing, not a curse.

The Apostle Peter tells us, "Dear friends, do not be surprised at the painful trial you are suffering, as though something strange were happening to you. But rejoice that you participate in the sufferings of Christ, so that you may be overjoyed when his glory is revealed. If you are insulted because of the name of Christ, you are blessed, for the Spirit of glory and of God rests on you."

Therefore, we saw beyond our sufferings and rejoiced in them.

After sunset, Colonel Haile ordered them to take me to my quarters. I laid down in my thatched-roof room, daydreaming and thinking. I especially kept thinking about the brothers' sufferings of which Habtom told me. Thinking about their steadfastness, I forgot my sufferings. In extreme suffering and pain, injustice and violence, it is in such times as these that the steadfastness of believers is revealed. This has borne fruit and has covered the earth.

In the twenty first century, the number of people who are enduring suffering for the sake of the gospel and for Christ is great. Some endure imprisonment, others bear suffering, some accept beatings, while others pay with their lives. Such devotion and sacrifice doesn't leave heroes of the faith without a reward. These people become capable where nothing is possible, and they spread an aroma of joy in the place of sadness. In the place that smells of death, they sow life. I felt very proud because I was counted as one of their number.

Dawn found me with a physically suffering body but with a revived spirit. One of my roommates, using pet name reserved for me called out and handed me a sealed letter. "Yesterday, while you were away someone brought you this," she told me.

Intrigued I began to open the envelope.

32

This Book has My Story

Without asking who brought me the letter, I opened the envelope. Before I started reading its contents, I began to scan its final page to find out who it was from. It was from my brother who was also suffering in Alaa. I wept for about half an hour.

The sister who handed me the letter rebuked me, "Why are you weeping before you have read its contents? Don't you think this saddens God? You taught us to glorify and thank God in all situations and at all times for what we have received. Have you forgotten that?"

I wiped away my tears, and began to read the letter. This was the contents of the letter:

"Dear Beloved, the one I love dearly, and God willing, whom I seek to see, lovely, beautiful, and a hero of the faith, whose belt is the Truth, and whom Satan can't defeat, whom the heat of Wia has not broken, the threats and intimidation of the enemies of Righteousness has not frightened, who has not capitulated in that place where Death's fumes rise, who has not exchanged her Saviour to escape hardship and injustice."

"Dear and beloved sister,

May the grace and peace be with you from God, our Father, and from our Saviour, Jesus. I am not going to ask you the usual question as I am experiencing the same things, and I know how you are. Do you remember what we used to say to each other as we studied the Bible and prayed at home? Do you remember, you often used to tell us that 'We are known in Christ'? It is possible that due to extreme suffering and pain we might think that we have been completely forgotten, and that none would remember us."

"Dear and beloved sister, despite all the injustices we are experiencing, we are still remembered in Christ."

"Sometimes I remember you and our family, and my inside feels saddened, and this weakens me. But later, I remember the promises of God, and like David I tell my soul, 'O my Soul, why do you disturb me? Put your hope in God, your saviour.'"

"Now, our family is scattered due to the sufferings that attacked it. Loneliness has engulfed it, and it is so deathly quiet. One day this loneliness will be replaced by eternal shouts of joy and laughter, and our souls will not be overwhelmed by the hardships they have borne. There is season for hardship, a season for laughter and embracing may come. Who can tell?"

"One day, our uncle, the colonel, came to give me a visit. He was enraged and told me, 'You criminals! Look what you have done to the family! Everyone is gone!' Shall I tell you what I answered him, dear sister? 'The righteous are not destroyed, but they bloom!' It was he who told me about our mother's condition."

"Sometimes, I think God is very cruel, and I blame him in my heart. Later, however, I cry bitterly: 'O God! And now, my mother?' But God has not made any mistake in all his deeds. I tell myself, 'God is righteous. And he knows what He does.' And I rejoice having overcome the darkness that had surrounded me."

"Our mother has been ill since our father's death. As a matter of fact, if you consider her situation, it is beyond measure. She is a mother. In fact, it is God's grace that she still bears it all. It is not easy. While we were in Asmara, she thought we wouldn't come back alive when we left home. Now, when I think how she bore it, I am amazed by the grace and mercy of God. Our uncle told me that a doctor had told her that she had kidney problems. He also told me that she had been advised to get medical care abroad because her illness could not be treated here."

"But, where can the money come from for medical care abroad? Though she stayed alive by taking medicine, she felt worse. Some Christians (God bless them) contributed some money and sent her to the Sudan. Our eldest sister went with her to the Sudan. However, according to uncle, her kidneys failed, and she is having dialysis. She is still not doing well according to uncle. However, nothing is impossible for God. Let us continue to pray for her. God may perform a miracle on her behalf, if that is His will."

"Uncle also told me that our sister got engaged in the Sudan. God has been good to her. I am telling you such news because I don't want you to trouble yourself asking, 'How are they?' Instead, I want you to get informed and start praying."

"If it is about me, I don't have much information to share, for

I experience the same things you do. Since there is a verse that states, 'God has made everything good in its time,' perhaps God will make an end to the sufferings we are experiencing."

"I want to advise you this. I want to impress this in your mind. Let's stand in the faith even though our suffering is hard. Our hope is Jesus Christ."

"To be honest, for faith to be tested like gold, it has to pass through different kinds of hardships. However, even if we pass through the valley of the shadow of death, God is with us. The fleeting hardships which we see, are proof that God is with us. Therefore, stand strong and stand in the faith. If it is God's will to give us a second opportunity, we will meet again and will declare God's mercy. If that is not the case, we will meet again in that eternal place where there are no trials and tribulations. I love you very much, and I have great respect for you. No one can separate us from the love of Christ. From your younger brother."

After I finished reading it, I felt as if I had an electric shock and went numb. My mind began to wander here and there. The letter that was in my hand was about one year old. Why did I receive the letter after almost a year? Only God knows. Is my mother dead? Or is she still alive? Is my sister married? How about my brother, has he been released? I felt in my heart that our house, which experienced laughter all the time, had become quiet and had been enveloped in a cloud of longing.

The sea of longing, sadness, and loneliness filled my heart.

After some hours, I quietly asked the sister who gave me the letter who had given it to her. The sister told me that a soldier brought it. She told me that he had told her that if I wanted, I could write a reply, since he was coming back after three weeks.

I decided in my heart to seize the opportunity given to me.

The hardcover notebook in which I put down my thoughts since I was imprisoned had almost run out of space. Now, it had only about ten leaves. It surprises and amazes me to see that this book in which I am writing my story has not fallen into the hands of my torturers or that it has not been lost during the time of my suffering. Who knows if my story would be a source of comfort and blessing for others?

In such hardship and suffering, the most troubling feeling is that the people who are not in similar situations do not care about you and may even have forgotten you. Sometimes when the situation gets pitch dark and when I think of my future, I find it hard to endure, "Where are my friends? Those who shared the same meal as me? Those people who prayed and sang with me, do they remember me?" I ask disturbed. Later, I say to myself, "If it had not been for the prayers of my brothers and sisters, I wouldn't have overcome the trouble I am experiencing."

The longing we experience to see our families and friends during times of trouble is very bitter. When my soul and the souls of my fellow Christians are hit by loneliness, we derive comfort from the laughter and songs we sang among many brothers and sisters.

Due to our faith in the Lord, we are considered as garbage, and we have lost all our possessions. But in Heaven, we have a place that cannot be taken away from us, and this comforts us and helps us endure beyond the sores of our affliction.

I have seen my soul rescued from death by a narrow escape. I have seen my fellow Christians die before my eyes. I have sought death many times. Reasonably, death is much preferred than this condition I am in. But what if God wanted me to tell the story of His heroes?

The years which I would have used productively and could have used to lay the foundations of my future life, I have spent in Sawa, Wia, and Mietir. It is very difficult and very unbearable.

The most amazing thing is that I don't regret the decision I have taken to give myself to suffering for the gospel. I don't know when I will be released from this injustice. However, God, who has given me his promise, doesn't lie and doesn't forget his promises.

I know I will see my Saviour one day whether that is after death or in life. I say with Job "I know that my redeemer lives, and that in the end he will stand on the earth. And after my skin has been destroyed, yet in my flesh I will see God; I myself will see him with my own eyes—I, and not another. How my heart yearns within me!" It is not the hardship and suffering that I experience and receive on my body, but God's love and mercy which I recall above my sufferings. In the years of my past experience, I have learned that God's grace and His glory are above my suffering and pain.

One afternoon, the sister who received the letter and gave it to me told me that the man who delivered the letter had come to see me, but because conditions were not conducive he would have to return another time. I told the sister, "I don't know why, but my heart is filled with the desire of Heaven. The day before yesterday at about dawn, I spent the night with my father in my dream."

The sister replied, "Don't think about Heaven yet. You have just started God's work and haven't finished it. If you are gone, who will relate your sufferings?"

I told her, "Do you see this book? All my story is written in that book. If that is God's will, I will give the brother the book with the letter. It is not only my story and the story of suffering. Since it is the story of steadfastness and history, it will be a lesson for many people."

The next morning, two soldiers came to the thatched roof house, and informed me that I was wanted. In my heart I said, "Where am I going this time?"

"We will come back after one hour. Pack all your clothes and get ready!" They gave me a stern warning. I told the sister who was with me, "I don't know where I am going. I also don't know what they will do with me. Therefore, please give the man who is coming to collect my letter to my brother this book containing my story."

Up to this hour, I am still suffering under difficult hardship and injustice. God willing, if I survive my sufferings, I will continue the story of my struggles. If, on the other hand, it is God's will that I should go home, be strong in the Lord and His might until we meet in Heaven again.

Finally, I would like to make one request: "Please, remember us! Pray for us! Be our supporters in this time of trial!"

The End

Additional information

Amensty International's video on the network of prisons in Eritrea: https://www.youtube.com/watch?v=pt8ST1U4o60&feature=youtu.be

Amensty Internaltional's interactive map of the network of secret detention centers in Eritrea: https://aiusa.maps.arcgis.com/apps/OnePane/basicviewer/index.html?appid=11f3f838f42144b39ddabe125ec82846